BEARING
THE
SPIRIT'S FRUIT

An Inspirational Perspective For
Managing Relationships

DANIEL EMAH

THE
CORNERSTONE
PUBLISHING

BEARING THE SPIRIT'S FRUIT:
An Inspirational Perspective For Managing

Paperback ISBN: 978-1-952098-08-6

Published by:
Cornerstone Publishing
A Division of Cornerstone Creativity Group LLC
Info@thecornerstonepublishers.com
www.thecornerstonepublishers.com
516.547.4999

Author's Contact
For speaking engagement or to order books by Daniel Emah please email: danema7@gmail.com

CONTENTS

Dedication

To God Almighty who has made it possible for me to declare His counsels among men in my generation. To Him alone be the glory forever and ever. Amen.

Acknowledgments

I appreciate my late elder brother, Elder Silas Sidi Emah, who laid a good Christian foundation for me, having become my foster father at age six. Unfortunately, Elder Silas was called to glory at the time I was writing this book. He will forever be fondly remembered.

I also thank God for my elder brother, Pastor Emmanuel Emah, who stood by me at every stage in my faith walk. I am most grateful to my precious, God-given wife, Gloria Emah, my wonderful provider of strength in time of weakness. I am very proud of our wonderful children: Favor, Shama, Japhet, Jireh and Phoebe, who continue to make sacrifices for us to do the master's work.

My wonderful appreciations go to my spiritual leader and mentor, Pastor Anthony Odugunwa, in whom I found certain levels of all the concepts that are discussed in this book. His lifestyle and teaching will ever remain a blessing to me and many others that he has mentored. Pastor Anthony has raised the bar of humility far beyond the reach of his contemporaries.

I appreciate my cousin, General J.A Adejo who has been a motivator that transformed my story to Bearing the spirit's fruit. Thank you sir for taking time to do the first line of proof reading.

Many thanks to Reverend A.O. Ocheje for doing the second line of proof reading. I appreciate your generous contributions and imput.

Last but not the least, I want to thank my publisher, Pastor Gbenga Showunmi and his team of editors who are not just book publishers, but a team of vision developers for their professionalism in making bearing the spirit's fruit the book of choice.

Above all, I am grateful to God, who made the provision for my salvation and has kept me in faith, despite my daily imperfections.

Foreword

This book, *Bearing the Spirit's Fruit,* is a must-read for every believer on the journey to spiritual maturity. It talks about the different components of the fruit of the Spirit. Pastor Dan Emah, a seasoned teacher of the word, creates a spiritual atmosphere needed to triumph in the Christian journey. The Kingdom principle is that of living and manifesting the fruit of the Spirit.

This book has the right ingredients to grow a healthy Christian life, while projecting Jesus Christ to the world. Pay close attention to every chapter of this book, learning godly principles and simplistic tools to make anyone grow a healthy Christian life. The Church of Jesus Christ has left her first love; it's time for us to revisit the beginning and flourish while awaiting the coming of the Savior.

Our world would be less polluted if the principles of the Scripture are gladly accepted and lived out by every Christian. If you desire to live a healthy Christian life, *Bearing the Spirit's Fruit* is highly recommended for you. This book will equip you not only for this world but for the world to come.

Pastor Anthony B. Odugunwa
The Redeemed Christian Church of God
Mount Zion Parish

Lake City Georgia, USA

Introduction

Bearing the Spirit's Fruit is an exposition on the fruit of the Spirit, as described in Galatians 5. The most economic importance of a tree is its fruit. The Bible also shows us the importance of fruit bearing, especially with strict warnings on the danger of trees not bearing fruits. In Matthew 3:10, Jesus Himself declared, *"And now also the axe is laid unto the root of the trees: therefore every tree which bringeth not forth good fruit is hewn down, and cast into the fire."*

Every believer is a spiritual economic tree that is expected to bear fruits as Returns on Investment (ROI). As economic entities in God's kingdom, we believers occupy an economic space, and if we are not productive, chances are that we may lose this space.

I used to be a peasant farmer with a little garden at the back of my home. In my garden, I grew vegetables and other crops. Any crop I planted and tended with proper care, but which refused to bear fruits, I cleared out with the weeds so that I didn't have to deal with it competing with other fruit-bearing crops for the soil's nutrients. This is a natural recourse for every farmer, as no farmer is ever happy about trees not bearing fruits.

In Jesus' parable of the fig tree in Luke 13, the owner of a vineyard instructed the vineyard dresser to cut down a fig tree that had been fruitless for three years. *"He spake also this parable; A certain man had a fig tree planted in his vineyard; and he came and sought fruit thereon, and found none. Then said he unto the dresser of his vineyard, Behold, these three years I come seeking fruit on this fig tree, and find none: cut it down; why cumbereth it the ground?"*

Owing to the experience I had garnered from tending my little backyard farm, when I was inspired to write about the Fruit of the Spirit, it was not difficult getting to it; and with little research, I was good to go. Jesus Christ also described His Father as the Gardener, as I was to my garden. *"I am the true vine, and my Father is the husbandman (gardener). Every branch in me that beareth not fruit he taketh away: and every branch that beareth fruit, he purgeth it, that it may bring forth more fruit"* (John 15:1, 2).

As God's express image, we believers take economic decisions by default, like I did in my backyard garden to optimize my little space. We are plants in God's garden, and He makes huge investments in us, with the expectations of getting returns on His investments in terms of the fruit we bear. So, God comes to us as His garden from time to time with His pruning chisel, to prune the fruitful plants and remove the fruitless ones.

As you read this book, it is my prayer that God will grant you understanding of the implication of fruitlessness, to avoid being a victim of same. May you choose to be fruitful and enjoy continuous pruning by the tender Gardener. If you are fruitful, you continue to enjoy nutrient supply from God. However, if you stop being fruitful for too long, not only does He stop supplying you, He removes you to maximize space and nutrients.

At a time, when I discovered that I was losing so many plants and space in my garden, I thought of how to tackle the challenge. Then I remembered the grafting technique and applied it to save the plants, and by so doing, optimized my space. What I did was to cut the buds of the fruitful plants and implanted them into the fruitless plants to make them fruitful. This method of grafting in agriculture is similar to what God does in the life of an individual at conversion.

When an individual becomes born again, he is spiritually engrafted into God's family. From this point, he continues to receive nourishment from God and is expected to start bearing fruit as soon as possible. This is a general principle of God's kingdom. Every fruit-bearing plant continues to enjoy a steady supply of God's favor, abundant life, eternal life and reward at the end of life, while those that do not bear fruits will struggle through a life of scarcity and lack while waiting for eternal condemnation.

Naturally, every plant in a garden is expected to bear fruits to justify its existence, except it is infected with a disease. In the same way, we were all destined for fruitfulness in the garden of God but got infected with sin and lost the ability to bear fruit. But, of His own will, God engrafted His productive capacity in us at salvation to assume our original fruit-bearing capacity. When the Spirit of God takes over your life, you will begin to produce fruit as evidence. *"But the fruit of the Spirit is love, joy, peace, longsuffering, gentleness, goodness, faith, Meekness, temperance: against such there is no law"* (Galatians 5:22, 23).

Bearing the Spirit's Fruit is the inspirational analysis of this Scripture with emphasis on its importance in successful and victorious Christian living. I carefully analyzed each component of the fruit as it affects different areas of human endeavor. This book will be very useful as a teaching guide for Christian teachers, as well as for marriage and family counseling.

CHAPTER 1

THE SUPREMACY OF LOVE

"Biblical love is not emotions or feelings, but attitudes and actions that seek the best interests of the other person, regardless of how we feel toward him." —**Jerry Bridges**

It is both interesting and instructive that the first component of the fruit of the Spirit mentioned in Galatians 5:22-23 is love. Love is God in action, and it is naturally the most distinctive attribute of anyone who has been regenerated by the Holy Spirit. Moreover, every other component of the fruit of the Spirit can be said to be an offshoot of love. As Evangelist D.L. Moody once explained, "Joy is love exalted; peace is love in repose; long-suffering is love enduring; gentleness is love in society; goodness is love in action; faith is love on the battlefield; meekness is love in school; and temperance is love in training."

You may have noticed already that the love I am referring to here is of a special kind. It is beyond human imagination. It goes beyond a deep affection for someone for whatever reason. It transcends reason, time and circumstances. This is why no one can truly manifest such dimension of love without having the nature of God engrafted in them.

Just imagine an attorney who is willing to change the verdict of a criminal condemned to death, grant him total freedom, eternal immunity - and to do this without expecting any reward? That is the kind of love I am talking about here. *"For God so loved the world, that he gave his only begotten Son, that whosoever believeth in him should not perish, but have everlasting life. For God sent not his Son into the world to condemn the world; but that the world through him might be saved"* (John 3:16-17). God desires to bear all our pain, so that we can enjoy eternal bliss and rest.

It is only God who can grant mercy at His own expense. He paid the ultimate price for our freedom from the conviction and penalty of offense against Him. When we transgress the law of God, we offend Him and are separated from Him, spiritually speaking. Love is an act of God, bringing man from condemnation back to Himself. Indeed, our justification was bought with the price denominated in the love of God. His love for us constrained Him to give His only begotten Son to purchase our eternal justification and it is His desire for us to live in love. Little wonder Jesus Himself in Matthew 22:40, said in no uncertain terms that the greatest of the commandments is to genuinely love God and our fellow men.

The acceptable love according to the response of Christ in the above verse is two-directional: love towards God and love towards man (neighbor). In other words, if you claim to love God, you must have love for your neighbor by default. Christ is the symbol of love and if He lives in you, your activities and relationships will manifest Him. The moment you encounter Christ and you allow Him room to dwell inside of you, you begin to express His qualities, first among which is love.

The manifestation of love in a Christian is like the biological expression of genes. If you acquired the genes for a light skin complexion from your parents, you must be a light-skinned person. Now, that said, unlike humans, when Jesus Christ came to earth as a man, He had only one gene, because His biological formation did not happen through fertilization between two human cells. The Spirit of God (Love) was incubated in a virgin woman and was born in

17

human form. As hard as this may be to believe, it is the naked truth about God.

Recall that God created the world and everything in it with the words of His mouth. In coming to earth, it would therefore have been easy for Him to reproduce Himself in flesh form or through any means He so desired; but the simple fact that He chose to come to the world through virgin conception and birth is a pointer that He preferred a purified environment void of any form of sin and that whoever accepts Him must seek to live a life of purity.

Because God, in love, paid the price to reconcile lost humanity to Himself, He wants us to relate with Him in love, which He described as the greatest of all the commandments. He expects us to justify His love for us by living our lives totally in love for Him and toward our neighbors. As the Righteous Judge, God is fair in His judgment; He gave His only begotten Son to reconcile us to Himself. In the same way, He wants us to appreciate His love by loving Him in return with the totality of our hearts, our souls, and our minds. We express our appreciation of God's love towards us in worship and in service.

Let us examine the three dimensions of love towards God.

LOVING GOD WITH ALL YOUR HEART

This dimension of love towards God comes with a strong sense of affection and tenderness for God. The expression of this kind of love finds its drive in your knowledge and relationship with Him. Loving God with all your heart takes you to the realm of life where no circumstance can affect your absolute loyalty to Him. Your love for God at this realm makes you believe His words to the letter and abide in Him. Apostle Paul was an example of New Testament believers who expressed this realm of love towards God: *"Who shall separate us from the love of Christ? shall tribulation, or distress, or persecution, or famine, or nakedness, or peril, or sword? As it is written, For thy sake we are killed all the day long; we are accounted as sheep for the slaughter. Nay, in all these things we are more than conquerors through him that loved us. 38 For I am persuaded, that neither death, nor life, nor angels, nor principalities, nor powers, nor things present, nor things to come, Nor height, nor depth, nor any other creature, shall be able to separate us from the love of God, which is in Christ Jesus our Lord"* (Romans 8:35-39).

Like Paul, we need to allow the love of God to influence our judgments, no matter the circumstances. If Christ died for us to live, then not even death should be able to interfere with our absolute loyalty and dedication to the service of God. He considered that if Christ died for our redemption and reconciliation to God, it is not fair for us to deny Him even in the face of death. A lot of us have denied Christ several times and under different circumstances. Most of the time, our denial of Christ happens before we know it, like in the case of Apostle Peter.

Once upon a time, I was in dire need of a job and I had a professional prepare a resume for me with false claims of experiences. As soon as the resume was put online, I started getting invitation for interviews. I had the knowledge to pass all kinds of written and oral interviews, but I did not have the experience. I almost got one job offer, but within me was a very heavy sense of guilt and condemnation to the extent that I was literally losing my sleep. I mentioned the situation to my wife, and she said a lot of people do not start jobs with experience, but the kind of job I am talking about was advertised for experienced professionals. Like Peter, my judgment was beclouded by my situation at that material time. I had to call the employers that I was not qualified for the position, in terms of experience, before I could regain my peace and joy. Today, I thank God that I did not allow that situation to separate me from the love of God.

Sometimes the way we come into a relationship with Christ influences our love for God. The way Peter was called was easier than the way Paul was drafted.

Peter was honorably invited, but Paul was struck, convicted and forcefully drafted. It was easier for Peter to be separated from the love of God than Paul. When your foundation is based on "anything goes", you may be vulnerable to situations separating you from the love of God. Always dare to say like Paul, *"What mean ye to weep and to break mine heart? for I am ready not to be bound only, but also to die at Jerusalem for the name of the Lord Jesus"* (Acts 21:13). Paul was ready to move from his comfort zone for the sake of Christ. He was able to overcome the threats of death by his resilient and uncompromising stance in declaring his undying love for God.

Any statement founded on the love of God overcomes situations because God's presence is in His words. If you speak to situations based on the love of God, He is invited into the situation to work in your favor. When you love God with all your heart, you will not have any room in your life for sentiments to thrive and weaken you. The opposition to the Gospel during Paul's time attempted to use sentiments as a weapon to weaken him, but his total love for Christ gave him the strength to make a statement of determination that not even death could stop him from loving God and boldly declaring the gospel of Jesus Christ.

The moment Paul made this statement of victory, I imagine him gaining his freedom from fear instilled by his associates who were advising him to slow down to avoid the danger of persecution by the opposition. The worst persecution that has ever happened to man is death and he was ready to die for righteousness sake. Paul was literally unstoppable. He was very resolute in his determination to stand for God, even in the face of stiff opposition and possible death, because he loved God *with all his heart*, meaning that he placed God above self.

Paul acknowledged that everything about him was for God, so it was easier for him to make a difference in his ministry. When you truly encounter God, and you accept him into your life, He becomes your life and everything about you reflects Him from that moment: *"I am crucified with Christ: nevertheless I live; yet not I, but Christ liveth in me: and the life which I now live in the flesh I live by the faith of the Son of God, who loved me, and gave himself for me"* (Galatians 2:20). Paul was saying that he used to live a life in perpetual slavery to sin and guilt, but God paid for his justification and freedom, and as a result, he has chosen to dedicate his life to Him.

A choice to let God into your life to live it for you is as wise as hiring the manufacturer of your car as your driver; as long as he/she is your driver, you are guaranteed a sound and healthy car. This is exactly what happens to us when we handover our lives totally to God, we are guaranteed a smooth ride in life; from labor to favor, from pain to gain, from shame to fame, from begging to giving, from picking to gleaning, from horror to honor, from intimidation to invitation, from pity to pretty.

However, the moment you fire this driver, he leaves with all these skills you have been enjoying. This is what happens with someone who falls back into sin, Christ the driver of your life is sacked by sin because He wants the totality of your love and your heart, for He is too pure to co-habit your life with sin. When sin fires Christ, it hires Satan the devil; and unlike God, the manufacture of your life who guarantees you a smooth ride and a healthy car, you begin to experience the reverse until ultimate death; from favor to labor, from gain to pain, from fame to shame, from giving to begging, from gleaning to picking, from honor to horror, from invitation to intimidation, from pretty to pity.

The worst choice to make in life is to give room for both God and Satan in your life, because it cannot be. One will try to prevail over the other in control of your life and you will crash like a car with two drivers fighting over the same wheel. *"No man can serve two masters: for either he will hate the one, and love the other; or else he will hold to the one, and despise the other. Ye cannot serve God and mammon"* (Matthew 6:24).

I like the way Dr. Myles Munroe analyzed this verse. He said there are two masters ruling this world; God and money. In the political world, people seek powers to have money as opposed to serving people to the glory of God, and in the religious world, people seek leadership positions either to serve money or God. It is a thing of serious concern for religious leaders who are supposed to lead their followers to God to fall short of serving God wholeheartedly. We can understand why politicians seek power to enrich themselves rather than serve the people; God is not brought into the equation.

Mind you, God is not interested in sharing His glory with anyone: *"I am the LORD: that is my name: and my glory will I not give to another, neither my praise to graven images"* (Isaiah 42:8). The Scriptures cannot be broken, and God does whatever He says. It therefore means that a lot of Christian leaders serving God and money have long walked God out of their lives. Could you imagine the magnitude of futility staring you in the face, if you are worshiping under a leader that is a servant to money? It is hard for you to grow spiritually because you are not learning spiritual values to enhance your growth.

Let me quickly chip in that God has made man a free moral agent and does not impose Himself on our choice. If you choose to serve money, God withdraws for money to take total charge. And when you start loving money, it begins to dictate to you what to do as a master does to a servant. It is written; *"For the love of money is the root of all evil: which while some coveted after, they have erred from the faith, and pierced themselves through with many sorrows"* (1 Timothy 6:10). When money takes over your heart, you begin to prefer material growth to spiritual growth and your congregation is afflicted with the spirit of materialism. Where materialism prevails, there is always pride, competition and ego (edging God out).

The sad reality is that where materialism prevails, people do not observe their spiritual obligations like giving and tithing, positioning themselves for perpetual lack. Somebody said if you begin to chase money it will run from you. I am speaking from my personal experience as a pastor; because we don't want to lose a member that is a giver, we indirectly make him or her a dictator of some sort or master of the pastor. So, they dictate the sermons we preach as opposed to the message from God. These masters have itching ears and are always in search of sermons that massage their larger than life ego. They are also very skillful in evangelizing and making disciples of themselves.

When these moneybag masters infiltrate the church with their pride and vain glory, they begin to edge out godly members by default, leaving the church with a large congregation filled with a bunch of people whose god is their belly, all thronging the broad and fast-paced road to hell. It is written: *"Enter ye in at the strait gate: for wide is the gate, and broad is the way, that leadeth to destruction, and many there be which go in thereat: Because strait is the gate, and narrow is the way, which leadeth unto life, and few there be that find it"* (Matthew 7:13-14). It is by far more rewarding to raise few members that will go to heaven than raising a multitude that will go to hell.

A church that is mastered by money produces lust-driven members instead of love-driven ones. *"Be not deceived; God is not mocked: for whatsoever a man soweth, that shall he also reap. For he that soweth to his flesh shall of the flesh reap corruption; but he that soweth to the Spirit shall of the Spirit reap life everlasting"* (Galatians 6:7-8). It is impossible to sow lust and reap love. In a lust-driven church, there is division and discrimination - mostly along racial, ethnic, or sectional lines - motivated by mere social support system, rather than genuine love. In a lust-driven church, people of like manner gather themselves together to gossip instead of fellowship, turning the church into a theatre of hatred, strife, and contention over recognition.

The devil is always happy with a lust-driven church because he is winning, for in the absence of love, he accomplishes his mission; *"Now the works of the flesh are manifest, which are these; Adultery, fornication, uncleanness, lasciviousness, Idolatry, witchcraft, hatred, variance, emulations, wrath, strife, seditions, heresies, Envyings, murders, drunkenness, revellings, and such like: of the which I tell you before, as I have also told you in time past, that they which do such things shall not inherit the kingdom of God"* (Galatians 5:19-21).

When a church is led by a leader who is mastered by money, the members will manifest the evils described in the passage above and when the church is corrupted by the love of money, instead of love for God, the community and the world at large is corrupt. The Bible describes the Body of Christ as the judge of the world and if the judge is corrupt, the clients will be corrupt to be able to work with him. Most people who truly possess the power of God are not recognized, because they are not money people and what you see today in most churches is the spirit of money rather than the Spirit of God.

Do not get me wrong; money is good. In fact, I call it "the driving wheel of the gospel." Just like you are in control of the wheel of the car to get to your destination, you (the gospel) are in charge of money to take you to your destination. Do not be confused that I call you the gospel; clearly *"ye are manifestly declared to be the epistle of Christ ministered by us, written not with ink, but with the Spirit of the living God; not in tables of stone, but in fleshy tables of the heart"* (2 Corinthians 3:3).

Money is very important to the gospel, but it is very wrong to allow it to control the gospel. As important as the wheel may be to the driver, it will be disastrous when it starts to control the driver. Instead of going where the driver wants it, the wheel will take the driver where it pleases. The unfortunate thing is that when you are controlled by money as a pastor, you lose the leadership and provision by God. When you are doing the work of God and you are totally under His control, you are guaranteed the provisions to successfully carry out your assignment. The provisions of God for His loyal servants are; protection, prosperity in wealth and health, happy marriage and family life, favor and every good thing; because it is written: *"But seek ye first the kingdom of God, and his righteousness; and all these things shall be added unto you"* (Matthew 6:33).

The problem with many Christians is that we take more time to talk about God's words than doing it. Unfortunately, the reward is in the doing, not the talking. It is hard for you to find a Christian who cannot recite this passage, *"But he that heareth, and doeth not, is like a man that without a foundation built an house upon the earth; against which the stream did beat vehemently, and immediately it fell; and the ruin of that house was great"* (Luke 6:49); but few Christians are doing it and it is a strong weapon the devil wields against the Kingdom of God.

When you are a doer of God's word, you enjoy His insurance, which protects your works from destruction by the devil. When you decide to listen, or heed the word of God, you become a possible threat to the devil, and he will be ready to attack. At the doing level of the word, the devil will attempt to attack, but he will fail because you will be indemnified by the insurance policy of God. When you are a doer of God's word, He takes care of your enemies before they start manifesting. The account in 2 Chronicles 20:17-23 tells us how God laid ambush against the children of Ammon, Moab, and mount Seir until they destroyed themselves when they came together in cohort against Judah.

God that did that then is the same God. He has not changed, not even your situation can change Him. He is the Unchanging Changer, the great I Am. He was I Am in the days of Jehoshaphat; He is I Am today, and He will forever be I Am. My unchanging God will take your battle to your enemies' camps and give you victory.

Like Jehoshaphat, you need to act on the word when you are confronted by a battle of any magnitude. When you are a policy holder against any hazard, you contact your insurer when the risk occurs to make your claims. When you are a loyal employee of God, He provides you a comprehensive coverage. All you are expected to do is contact God when you are threatened with any battle and He takes the battle right to the enemy's camp. The Israeli army under General Jehoshaphat did not have to get into face-to-face combat with their enemies to defeat them. Jehoshaphat contacted his policy carrier (God) to process his claims and the result was his victory over his enemies. The Lord God Himself will fight all your battles and give you victory over your enemies as you work for him rather than for money in Jesus' mighty name.

LOVING GOD WITH ALL YOUR SOUL

Time and again, people are referred to as souls in the Bible. According to the revelation of the Holy Spirit through different men He inspired to document the Scripture, the soul is that part of man that, unlike the body, does not suffer decay; it lives on forever (Matthew 10:28). The soul is also the seat of emotions. It is the emotional part of man with the sense of feeling and sentiments. God expects His children to sacrifice their feelings and sentiments and serve Him with all their soul. The ultimate price Christ paid for our salvation purchased the total man, therefore any service that is not done in total surrender is unacceptable to God.

The love of God that purchased our redemption is void of emotions and sentiments. When you determine to be saved, you surrender everything about you to God including your right to emotions and sentiments. A transformed individual is no longer responsive to feeling and sentiments because he has given up the old life and embraced the new life in Christ. He is dead to the old man of sin, has been buried with and resurrected with Christ. *"Therefore if any man be in Christ, he is a new creature: old things are passed away; behold, all things are become new"* (2 Corinthians 5:17).

The core evidence of salvation is forgiveness. The salvation of our soul is based on the forgiveness of our sins through God's love. When you are genuinely saved, you acquire the forgiving nature of God as an evidence; but if you are struggling with forgiveness as a Christian, then you need to check your salvation. Some Christians even say they can forgive but cannot forget. We need to realize that the offense that is not forgotten is as good as not forgiven. A transformed life does not remember offences that are forgiven because such an individual carries the nature of God. God is love and love forgives unconditionally. *"For I will be merciful to their unrighteousness, and their sins and their iniquities will I remember no more"* (Hebrews 8:12).

Here's what I believe the love of God really means: Leave old verdict and ease up. I derived this statement from the four letters that spell the word love as follows, **L**eave **O**ld **V**erdict and **E**ase up. The old verdict is condemnation and death for sin, but justification and redemption are the new verdict made available by grace through faith; *"For the wages of sin is death; but the gift of God is eternal life through Jesus Christ our Lord"* (Romans 6:23). The old verdict is of the law which spells condemnation and death for transgression, while the new verdict is grace for salvation and freedom. The principle that results in these two verdicts was designed by God to have a continuous relationship and fellowship with man. God's intention is not to destroy His original purpose for man with the new principle, but rather to reveal His purpose for man in His new principle (Grace/ Christ) for an everlasting relationship (Matthew 5:17-20).

Moreover, it takes transformation to have a peaceful marriage and a happy home. I have not heard of any marriage without challenges but love and forgiveness can walk you through all of them. Where there is genuine love, there is always forgiveness. I heard of a marriage that hit the rock because the wife felt the husband does not have feelings for her. The truth of the matter here is that, how you came together determines how long you will stay together. Feeling cannot replace love because it could be easily eroded by challenges and tests of life. The reason why most marriages fail soon after the wedding is because they are founded on feeling rather than love. Love is an attribute of God and it exists for ever just like God and it is patient and enduring; Love *"Beareth all things, believeth all things, hopeth all things, endureth all things"* (1 Corinthians 13:7).

As we have seen earlier, true love is two-way: towards God and towards neighbors; and since God works in an orderly manner, He requires us to love Him first so that loving others will be a walk in the park. There is therefore no love without God at the center and nothing can compete with Him at the center. From the narrative of the victim of this failed marriage, it is obvious that feeling, instead of love, was at the center of his marriage. When you first love God with all your soul; the very seat of emotion, feeling and sentiment, then He will condition you through the process of transformation to love others, because He is always looking for people through whom He can express His love to the world; *"Beloved, let us love one another: for love is of God; and every one that loveth is born of God, and knoweth God. He that loveth not knoweth not God; for God is love"* (1 John 4:7-8).

For any marriage to stand and be successful, both spouses must love God with all their soul first and God will bind them together in an unconditional love that cannot be broken by feelings. When you discover God and his love and determine to live for him, He will clean you up of your emotional and sentimental spirit and put His spirit in you to love unconditionally. You may be thinking that there are marriages that are standing without transformation experience, and I can assure you that if you are given the opportunity to counsel them, you will discover that they are enduring rather than enjoying it. You can only enjoy a marriage that is consummated in God and His love.

I was watching a television show about a couple who wanted to be sure of the father of their own child. I wondered how on earth they wanted to know the father of their own child. In the end, I discovered that they had legalized extra-marital affairs in their home to live happily together. This is a typical example of marriage that is driven by feelings rather than love. When the foundation of your marriage is laid on feelings, it will fail when the feelings die. I have seen many marriages hit the rocks because the couples misunderstood feelings for love. Love is the spirit of God indwelling the human heart, soul and mind; feelings on the other hand indwell the eye and the flesh. While feelings are based on perception, love is based on empathy.

In my growing years, I had always said I wanted to marry an attractive woman; one whose skin color and body contour satisfied my desires. My definition of love was limited to my feelings; God was nowhere in the equation. This is just how many people got stuck with strange bedfellows. But, when I eventually came of age and found my wife, something happened, which changed my perception of marriage for the better. You see, before I met my wife, I had approached different ladies out of my own feelings. But, as soon as I found my wife, God spoke and changed my perception of love from mere attraction to a deep inner conviction by God. When I proposed to my wife after finding out that she was a Christian and loved God, and I could see that the family loved the ways of God, she had to travel to the city where the grandparents lived to inform them of my proposal. The grandfather said this to her: "The choice of husband or wife should not be based on outside attraction, but inner attraction." He said any attractive person is attractive to everybody.

I discovered that what keeps you in marriage and makes you enjoy it is the hidden value in you that is connecting to the corresponding value in your potential spouse. Inner value is not attractive to the eye, but to the heart, soul and mind that is saturated with the love for God. My message to the young people is to first love God with all their heart, soul, and mind, and after that they will be able to make informed marital decisions for a sustainable and a happy home. It is written; *"Trust in the LORD with all thine heart; and lean not unto thine own understanding. In all thy ways acknowledge him, and he shall direct thy paths"* (Proverbs 3:5-6).

Another thing the younger generation needs to realize is that successful marriage is based on similar values (the love of God) upheld by couples. It is true that people get married based on commonly cherished values that have nothing to do with the love of God, but majority of such marriages could not stand the test of time. Most of them became successful because they got saved down the line after marriage (not a recommended route). I advise that marriage should be sought between people of the same faith and belief system. Abraham got fully involved in the choice of wife for his son because he was well-informed of the implication of two strangers coming together in marriage. In today's marriages, most children would have taken their decision before they let their parents know. It was not so from the beginning.

"And Abraham was old, and well stricken in age: and the LORD had blessed Abraham in all things. And Abraham said unto his eldest servant of his house, that ruled over all that he had, Put, I pray thee, thy hand under my thigh: And I will make thee swear by the LORD, the God of heaven, and the God of the earth, that thou shalt not take a wife unto my son of the daughters of the Canaanites, among whom I dwell: But thou shalt go unto my country, and to my kindred, and take a wife unto my son Isaac" (Genesis 24:1-4). Abraham, the

father of faith was not referring to physical location, but shared values and beliefs as necessary factors for marriage. He was born and brought up in a small town called Urfa in the northern ancient city of Ur, far away from Canaan where Abraham was living at the time he wanted Isaac to get married. Abraham and Isaac his son must have seen beautiful women with promising potentials in Canaan, but they realized that commonly shared values could keep a marriage standing against challenges.

"Can two walk together, except they be agreed?" Asked the prophet in Amos 3:3. Agreement is made on common ground where decision is taken for the mutual interest of the parties involved in a win-win situation. Any marriage founded on commonly shared values will stand the test of time, because the couples are likely to take decisions based on shared values and will be committed to such decisions. Although Abraham was at Canaan at this time, he was raised with the values of Urfa, his hometown. Just because you are living in a place does not mean that you automatically share their values. You may be an immigrant in the United States, but you may not like the types of foods they eat or dresses they wear.

A lot of people from different parts of the world dress differently. Some people like dressing in corporate wears while others want to appear casually.

As easy as this value may be, it could cause divorce. Other examples like table manners are values that could tear marriages apart, while some eat with their fingers, others eat with cutleries. Imagine a couple eating together; one with fingers and the other with cutleries. I heard about a marriage that broke a few weeks after it was consummated, because one of the couples snored a lot, which made it impossible for the other to sleep. In some part of the world, it is required of the wives to bow when greeting their husbands or serving them food and drinks.

In marriage, there are lots of sacrifices to make and it is important to understand the value systems of your partner and determine which of your own values you can trade with your would-be spouse before you go into marriage agreement. There is always a problem with a square peg in a round hole or an old wine in a new wine skin. *"And no man putteth new wine into old bottles: else the new wine doth burst the bottles, and the wine is spilled, and the bottles will be marred: but new wine must be put into new bottles"* (Mark 2:22). This scripture implies that two different people raised in different value systems will find it difficult to work together in marriage. People from some part of the world don't eat foods not cooked by them, so they are good cooks, others only eat in restaurants, so they don't cook. Marriage between people with these different backgrounds will not last long.

The list of differences in value system cannot be exhausted, but there is a value system that can override all other value systems to make it possible for people of different backgrounds to successfully stay together in marriage and build happy homes. I am talking about marriage that is consummated in the love for God. Most of the successful marriages I have seen are those that both parties share the common value of love for God. Marriages that are based on love for God, retain the presence of God, and because God does not fail, the marriage will be successful. When you genuinely accept Christ as your Savior at salvation, your old value system is replaced with the new value system, and this time you are no longer under the influence of your worldly culture, but under God's Kingdom culture. At this time your hunger and search for marriage will be directed to the kingdom of God where people with the same values and passions like you are found.

If you feel that you are led to a lady that is not of the same faith with you as a Christian, I advise that you seek counsel before you get committed, because you may be infatuated into that relationship. Scripture admonishes, *"Be ye not unequally yoked together with unbelievers: for what fellowship hath righteousness with unrighteousness? and what communion hath light with darkness?"* (2 Corinthians 6:14). You need to be saved first before you can be led to God's choice for you in marriage. When God is involved in your marriage, He stays with you in the marriage to guarantee lasting success and happiness. My wife and I have been married for fifteen years and by the grace of God, the past fifteen years have been like a month because loving God has been our shared value that has made everything work together for our mutual interest. We do everything together, including crying and laughing without any shadow of doubts and mistrust. We are coherently bound by love, such that nothing is allowed to come in between us, not even our children. My mother in-law has been with us for the past ten years, but she is like a mother to both of us because we have proved to her that we are one.

LOVING GOD WITH ALL YOUR MIND

The mind is the center of consciousness, where the thought process is generated. When you love God with all your mind, all your thought process and intellectual awareness will be centered on God's love. The moment you are saved by the transforming grace of God in Christ, your priority in life becomes those things that are based on the love of God. The mind is the battle ground of life and the way you strategize it determines whether you will win or lose. It is written: *"For as he thinketh in his heart, so is he: Eat and drink, saith he to thee; but his heart is not with thee"* (Proverbs 23:7).

If you determine to be successful in life you will be unstoppable by anything that appears like failure on your way to success. Failure in my opinion is like a stop sign on your way to your destination. It protects you from crashing before you land. When you fail, it is not the time to give up, but the time to reflect. When you give up to failure, you remain a failure, but if you reflect, you will find your mistakes and improve on them as you progress to success. Winners never quit; they say. Whatever you are in life depends on the state of your mind, otherwise called mindset. It is written: *"Keep thy heart with all diligence; for out of it are the issues of life"* (Proverbs 4:23).

Anything you allow into your mind or your heart controls you and your relationship either with men or God. *"For they that are after the flesh do mind the things of the flesh; but they that are after the Spirit the things of the Spirit. For to be carnally minded is death; but to be spiritually minded is life and peace. Because the carnal mind is enmity against God: for it is not subject to the law of God, neither indeed can be. So then they that are in the flesh cannot please God"* (Romans 8:5-8). Life is a matter of continuous decisions and choices. If you subject your mind to lustful thinking, your behavior will be lustful. You cannot be in the club where naked women are dancing or be addicted to pornography and be better than a prostitute.

"Ye have heard that it was said by them of old time, Thou

shalt not commit adultery: But I say unto you, That whosoever looketh on a woman to lust after her hath committed adultery with her already in his heart" (Matthew 5:27-28). Every battle is won or lost in the mind before it manifests. Paul emphasized the importance of the mind and thought process to the Philippian church when he said; *"Finally, brethren, whatsoever things are true, whatsoever things are honest, whatsoever things are just, whatsoever things are pure, whatsoever things are lovely, whatsoever things are of good report; if there be any virtue, and if there be any praise, think on these things"* (Philippians 4:8). The state of the mind variously referred to as mindset determines the level of your success. When you love God with all your mind, your thought process will be informed of love, as described by Apostle Paul in this scripture.

Now, let us quickly consider loving your neighbor as yourself. We had established in our description of Christian perspective of love, *that it is the desire of God to bear the pain of humanity at His own cost.* God has, in His demonstration of love for the world, set a standard for human beings in relating with one another. *"Be ye therefore followers of God, as dear children; And walk in love, as Christ also hath loved us, and hath given himself for us an offering and a sacrifice to God for a sweetsmelling savour"* (Ephesians 5:1-2). For an individual to demonstrate this type of love, he or she must have the Spirit of God through salvation.

A natural man is always self-centered with the "me and my family syndrome." Loving your neighbor as yourself, goes beyond standing by him when the going is good to standing with him when the going gets tough.

"Charity suffereth long, and is kind; charity envieth not; charity vaunteth not itself, is not puffed up, Doth not behave itself unseemly, seeketh not her own, is not easily provoked, thinketh no evil; Doth not behave itself unseemly, seeketh not her own, is not easily provoked, thinketh no evil; Beareth all things, believeth all things, hopeth all things, endureth all things" (1 Corinthians 13:4-7). These attributes of love are what I refer to as the check list of perfection. I have never seen or heard of anyone who possessed these attributes except God and if you allow him in your life, then your deeds will be perfect. For example, God's love is towards both sinners and the righteous. *"But God commendeth his love toward us, in that, while we were yet sinners, Christ died for us"* (Romans 5:8). If God loves even sinners; His enemies, you should not have problems with loving your enemies as an imitator of God.

If you have the spirit of God in you, you will always want to have an offence reconciled for continuous relationship. Do not allow offense to separate you from the love of Christ because with the flesh, offence must come. I think it is not of God to withdraw your love from a member who falls into sin and is suspended by church leadership. This may worsen the situation instead of helping it, because the devil may have a good reason to convince the victim for total discipleship. Even the conventional criminal justice system provides the basic needs for the inmates. In my opinion, Christian suspension of members should be at the level of removal from activity privileges with continuous prayers for the victim until he or she is restored back into faith. *"We then that are strong ought to bear the infirmities of the weak, and not to please ourselves"* (Romans 15:1).

As a community, Christians are supposed to be the best support system the world could ever know, and nothing should stop us from supporting one another. *"Woe unto the world because of offences! for it must needs be that offences come; but woe to that man by whom the offence cometh!"* (Matthew 18:7). A lot of people are living with wrong perception of love because they lack understanding of the author and the source of it. Love is of God and for one to love, he or she must first know Him by faith in Christ's atoning work. *"Beloved, let us love one another: for love is of God; and everyone that loveth is born of God, and knoweth God. He that loveth not knoweth not God; for God is love"* (1 John 4:7-8).

The parable of the Good Samaritan as told by Jesus in Luke 10:25-37 gives us a clear understanding of what it means to love your neighbor as yourself.

Jesus had shared this parable when a lawyer tempted Him with the question, *"Teacher, what shall I do to inherit eternal life?"* Harmless as this question seemed, Jesus saw right through the lawyer's mischief and in His infinite wisdom asked the learned fellow what was written in the Laws and the Prophets and his ready response was, *"And he answering said, Thou shalt love the Lord thy God with all thy heart, and with all thy soul, and with all thy strength, and with all thy mind; and thy neighbour as thyself."* The lawyer possessed head knowledge that he must love God with all his heart and love his neighbor as himself if he hoped to inherit eternal life. But the next question he posed revealed that he only possessed head knowledge but did not keep the commandment as provided in the Laws and Prophets. *"And who is my neighbour?"* Asked the lawyer.

When Jesus finished telling the story of the Good Samaritan, it became clear to His audience who the Good Samaritan was – the man that showed mercy, not the priest (Bishop, Apostle, Pastor, Prophet, Evangelist) or the Levite (a Christian) but the man who showed mercy on the wounded traveler dispossessed of his valuables and left to die. When it comes to loving your neighbor as yourself, spiritual title or position does not matter. The true test of this quality is the indwelling nature of God in one's life. The man who showed mercy was nameless and faceless, as it were. He did not bear any big title, but he showed mercy to the wounded man. He cleaned up the victim, did a first aid treatment of some sort for him, took him to the hospital and paid the bills.

Truly speaking, the third person in this parable of the Good Samaritan is the neighbor; and Jesus commands us to do like the Good Samaritan. A lot of Christians are carried away by the pursuit of material things and wealth without paying attention to those in need. Most spiritual leaders prefer to have a big cathedral or drive in expensive cars at the expense of their poor members. I heard of a church whose member that was suffering from cancer asked for help and the church said they could not, because if they did, it would become a pattern for others. This response defies the purpose of the church which is love.

As we wrap up this chapter, let me unequivocally state that the best support system of every true worshipper of God is the church. *"And all that believed were together, and had all things common; And sold their possessions and goods, and parted them to all men, as every man had need. And they, continuing daily with one accord in the temple, and breaking bread from house to house, did eat their meat with gladness and singleness of heart, Praising God, and having favour with all the people. And the Lord added to the church daily such as should be saved"* (Acts 2:44-47). How much support and succor do you bring to believers around you? Do you love God with all your heart, soul, mind, and your neighbor as yourself? Think on these things.

CHAPTER 2

THE WELLSPRING OF JOY

"Christian joy is not a giddy, superficial happiness that can be devastated by illness, economic difficulties, broken relationships, or the countless other vicissitudes and disappointments of life. Instead, it flows from the deep, unshakable confidence that God is eternally in control of every aspect of life for the good of His beloved children." — **John MacArthur**

The English dictionary gives the definition of joy to mean the feeling of great pleasure and happiness. But joy, as revealed in Scripture, goes beyond mere feeling of pleasure and happiness to the hope and assurance of living profitably here on earth and having a grand homecoming when we all get to heaven. It is the empowering confidence that comes from the assurance that one is operating in the Kingdom of God right from here on earth. This kind of joy gives you the ability to walk through situations with a resilient spirit until victory is won.

I was on a construction site on a very humid day. Everybody around me was quiet because of the unfavorable weather and eagerly waiting for the setting of the sun. It was very strange for anyone under the same situation to be singing happily and wear a happy face. For me, it was the time for praising and worshipping God as an avenue to relieve me of the ongoing pressure. As I was singing and praising God, a strong loud voice echoed: "Daniel, are you okay?" He could not understand why anyone in his right mind would be that joyful. When I heard his voice, it was like he woke me up from a deep and peaceful sleep, because I was not feeling the severity of the weather. Why was it so? The presence of God shielded me from the discomfort occasioned by humidity of the weather.

God's Spirit in man produces joy that is beyond human comprehension; therefore I was not surprised that my colleague could not comprehend the reason behind my joy under the condition we found ourselves at that material time. This kind of joy is a component of salvation that is hidden from the unsaved. When Christ died for our redemption, He bore upon Himself our burden. So, at salvation, your burdens are lifted off of you at Calvary. See, just the understanding of this alone is enough to drive you joyful through all of life's challenging situations.

Paul and Silas understood this concept so much so that they offered praise and thanksgiving to God while they were in prison to the extent that their worship resonated with the heaven and the host of heavens invaded their situation and got them out. *"And at midnight Paul and Silas prayed, and sang praises unto God: and the prisoners heard them. And suddenly there was a great earthquake, so that the foundations of the prison were shaken: and immediately all the doors were opened, and every one's bands were loosed"* (Acts 16:25-26).

"For the kingdom of God is not meat and drink; but righteousness, and peace, and joy in the Holy Ghost" (Romans 14:17). When your sprit (God's nature) receives the signal of rebirth through salvation, you begin to experience an overflowing realm of joy beyond human imagination and comprehension. At this point, you are operating at the level of the kingdom citizenship with full benefit. God's kingdom benefit goes beyond mere eating and drinking to unspeakable peace and joy in the Holy Ghost. This was exactly what played out in my situation at the construction site. It is practically impossible for you to carry the

presence of God inside of you and harbor sorrow, because in His presence, there is fullness of joy.

"Thou wilt shew me the path of life: in thy presence is fulness of joy; at thy right hand there are pleasures for evermore" (Psalm 16:11). There is a way that leads to the presence of God where the fullness of joy abounds, the way of life. I call it the link way. If you choose to ride on this way and you abide, you are in good standing with God and you will spend your days in pleasure.

Joy as the Fruit of the Spirit has the power to heal. Yes, you read me right! Joy certainly has healing powers. The wisest man that ever lived, captured the healing power of Joy, when he said *"A merry heart doeth good like a medicine: but a broken spirit drieth the bones"* (Proverbs 17:22). Spontaneous healing takes place in the bodies of those who possess the joy of the Holy Spirit. Every element of sorrow and sighing is neutralized by the joy of the Spirit. When you see an individual that is not easily given to offence and is joyful in every situation, that one is manifesting the fruit of the Holy Spirit called joy. *"And the ransomed of the LORD shall return, and come to Zion with songs and everlasting joy upon their heads: they shall obtain joy and gladness, and sorrow and sighing shall flee away"* (Isaiah 35:10).

Joy empowers you to walk through tests and storms of life until victory is won. I discovered that there is no success in life without some level of failure, and what propels in the journey of success, despite many failures is Joy in the Holy Ghost. *Looking unto Jesus the author and finisher of our faith; who for the joy that was set before him endured the cross, despising the shame, and is set down at the right hand of the throne of God"* (Hebrews 12:2).

Jesus Christ, our Perfect Example was able to endure torture and humiliation on the cross because he saw the glory and joy beyond the cross. At the climax of His suffering and cruel reproach, Jesus ignored His physical circumstances and positioned Himself at the center of His Father's will; and at that moment, He began to experience great joy by the Holy Spirit. When this joy saturated His heart in the face of death, He offered prayers of forgiveness for those that hated Him without cause and who were responsible for His dark moments. The joy of the Holy Spirit takes you to the level that you don't hold offence against anybody, because all offences work together for good in your favor. Those that crucified Jesus did not realize that their action was going to make Him even more popular than He was. One of his major sin they said was, "He said he is the king of the Jews," but after the cross he became the King of the world ruling over kingdoms and nations. He is the most popular hero that the world has ever known.

The joy of the Holy Spirit sustained Jesus through his trying moments. When you are born again and your spirit becomes transformed, you become a joint heir together with Jesus, meaning you have the same inheritance with Him and can do anything and even greater things than he did while on earth. *"Verily, verily, I say unto you, He that believeth on me, the works that I do shall he do also; and greater works than these shall he do; because I go unto my Father"* (John 14:12). As our model and a mentor in faith, Christ has raised the bar by manifesting the joy in the Spirit even in the face of death. The joy of the Spirit produces the physical joy to enables you walk through situations into your destiny. It is the joy in the Spirit of Christ that led Him to shed His blood for the world to experience the joy of salvation.

At His birth, Christ was announced as the joy to the world. *"And the angel said unto them, Fear not: for, behold, I bring you good tidings of great joy, which shall be to all people"* (Luke 2:10). It takes joy to produce joy. It is joy on the inside (in the heart of man) that manifests on the outside. The tree of joy inside of a man produces the fruit of joy on the outside. Let me share my personal experience with you about what I have benefitted from the joy on my inside. Every breakthrough I have ever gotten in my spirit has been preceded by the witness of inner joy. I used to work as an independent contractor for a government agency and it used to be once in an exceedingly long while. But any time I woke up with my spirit overwhelmed with joy, I received a call to start a project. Every good news I had in my life always happened after experiencing overwhelming joy in my spirit. Little wonder the Scripture tells us about the well of salvation where everything we need to make life worth living has been provided by God. *"Therefore with joy shall ye draw water out of the wells of salvation"* (Isaiah 12:3).

I know a man who enjoyed protection from the wells of salvation when a religious opposition attempted in vain to have him killed. This event took place many years ago on one of the campuses in Africa. The opposition mobilized themselves in numbers on a fateful night, as they terrorized other religious groups on campus. The first room they attacked was that of the campus Christian Fellowship leader. After getting hold of him and putting their sword on his neck to slaughter him, they gave him an opportunity to either renounce his faith or be slaughtered and dropped from the third story of the apartment block where he lived. He suddenly started singing a hymn; "Praise the Lord, praise the Lord, let the earth hear His voice…" and that was the victory that helped him overcome his situation. As soon as the terrorists perceived the unusual joy all over their victim, they dropped their weapons and ran away. This must be the same Spirit in Christ *"... who for the joy that was set before him endured the cross, despising the shame ..."* (Hebrews 12:2).

This brother was ready to be killed for the cause of the Gospel of Jesus Christ because the joy of the Lord had taken all forms of fear away from him. This was to prove to his persecutors that not even death can separate him from the love of God. The joy of the Lord gives you the sense of worthiness to suffer persecution. *"My brethren, count it all joy when ye fall into divers temptations"* (James 1:2). You cannot live a life of freedom until you are ready to die. A life that is devoid of fear dwells in total freedom. Charles De Lint once said, "If you are not ready to die, then how can you live?"

Do you know what happened after the botched murder attempt on that campus Christian Fellowship leader? This will interest you, wait for it! After that victory, not only did the leader become untouchable, that singular event marked the end of religious terrorism on that campus. Hallelujah!!! You need the joy of the Holy Spirit to liberate you from all forms of fears because a life that is subjected to fear is literally dead. When you approach trials and difficulties from the place of joy, you are celebrating God in that situation with the understanding that victory for that situation has been won for you a long time ago, and that in itself will invite God into the situation. And when God steps right into your situation, victory is assured.

Sustaining joy in every situation is produced by patience and patience gives you perfection and completeness, making it impossible for you to lack anything good and ushering you into a life of abundance and overflow. *"My brethren, count it all joy when ye fall into divers temptations; Knowing this, that the trying of your faith worketh patience. But let patience have her perfect work, that ye may be perfect and entire, wanting nothing"* (James 1:2-4). While sorrow and discouragement in the face of trials manipulate you for a defeat, an attitude of joy because of your absolute faith in God actualizes your victory.

The joy of salvation drives away fear and produces boldness and courage to walk though situations of life and head for victory. This was the experience of the three Hebrew children that were held in Babylonian captivity under the reign of king Nebuchadnezzar. These three young men demonstrated absolute faith in God and tapped into the wells of salvation to draw enough joy that gave them boldness to defend their faith in front of the world's fieriest dictator at that time. This single act of these young men attracted the presence of God, which manifested in the form of His Son. And that brought on the performance of one of the most unbelievable occurrences in Old Testament history. The account is in Daniel 3:21-30.

Remember Jehoshaphat, king of Judah? He was another man who used joy as a weapon to obtain victory and delivered his kingdom from the perpetual threat of invasion by the Moabites and the ammonites. When the battle line was drawn and Jehoshaphat saw how physically helpless his kingdom was before the combined garrison of Ammon, Moab and Mount Seir, he tapped into the joy of the Lord that gave him the strength to present his well-articulated petition to the throne of God in prayers. God responded to his prayer immediately through an individual called Jahaziel, a Levite and assured them that the battle was His and that all they needed to do was to stand and see the salvation of the Lord.

Instead of taking on the Ammonites, the Moabites, and their allies in battle, the unbelievable happened when Jehoshaphat and his people stood and watched their enemies killing themselves. Notice that Jehoshaphat and his people were told to stand and see the salvation of the Lord. The word salvation means preservation or safety. The strategy with which to receive preservation or safety in times of insecurity and emergency is to be calm and still. Anxiety and worry in situations suppress your feeling of safety and victory, leaving you with the picture of defeat and failure. Jehoshaphat and the congregation of the people of Judah and Jerusalem ignored the ragging battle and started praising the God of victory, the Mighty Man in battle, and He gave them total victory that they never fought for (2 Chronicles 20:10-26).

Moreover, an attitude of joy amid trials and tribulations of life takes you from the point of lack and scarcity to that of abundance and overflowing treasures. A life of abundance is an integral inheritance that God deposited for His children in the well of salvation.

CHAPTER 3

THE PEACE THAT SURPASSES UNDERSTANDING

"Peace should be a hallmark of the godly person, first because it is a Godlike trait: God is called the God of peace several times in the New Testament. He took the initiative to establish peace with rebellious men" —**Jerry Bridges**

There are different opinions on what the term "peace" means. However, the one I consider most applicable to all situations describes peace as a stress-free state of security and calmness, resulting from the absence of fighting or war, with coexistence in harmony and freedom.

Take a moment to reflect on the key words in this definition: **stress free, security, calmness, absence of fighting or war, coexistence, harmony,** and **freedom.**

I have been around for quite a while, but I have not seen or heard of any individual or nation that claims to have met the requirements of this definition. But I have indeed read about a handful of people who met these conditions, and they attributed their ability to do so to God alone. It therefore makes sense to believe that it is possible to meet the requirement of this definition only when God is involved. *"Peace I leave with you, my peace I give unto you: not as the world giveth, give I unto you. Let not your heart be troubled, neither let it be afraid"* (John 14:27).

The peace that God gives cannot be compared with that which the world offers. From the scope of our definition of peace, nothing can offer you peace but God. Neither money nor wealth can offer you peace. You can confirm this from any rich person you know. I know a rich man who started a building project when I was in high school; after finishing, he will destroy and start all over again. He continued the cycle of building and pulling down up to the time I graduated from college. I think he lacked peace because peace gives stability and contentment.

I also heard the story of a man who married many wives to have peace, but never found peace in his life time. I have lost count of people who thought they would find peace in living in mansions or riding in expensive cars, but in the end, could not find peace. A song writer wrote in one of the verses of my most favorite gospel hymns; "There are millions in this world who are seeking the pleasures earthly things afford, but none can match the wondrous treasures that are found in Jesus Christ my Lord". It is important to realize that happiness or pleasure is not peace, neither is any of these indicatives of presence or absence of peace. If you're living in sin, you could have happiness and pleasure that are short-lived, but peace and joy come from righteousness, a gift from God by grace through faith. Just five minutes of illegal sex may offer you bodily pleasure or happiness for that long and leave you sorrowful for the rest of your lifetime. I know of people who had few minutes of sexual pleasure before marriage and lost their ability to reproduce children for the rest of their lives.

The purpose of God is for the world to dwell in perfect and continuous peace. The purpose of God for the world is incorporated into His creation. Man was created after all that he needed to give him enduring peace had been made available. Peace is only found when needs are met, especially that of social justice. Unfortunately, one of the most of unmet needs of humanity world over is that of social justice. Voices of ordinary people are no longer heard, resulting in resentment and unrest in the society. Unfortunately, victims of social injustice, see radicalism and terrorism as the only way to make their voices heard. Judging by the sequence of events at creation, God's intention is for us to have a peaceful world.

The first family was in the Garden of Eden where adequate provision for the needs of humanity was made. As a matter of fact, God is more interested in our peace than we are. The instruction that God gave to the first family not to eat of the fruit from a tree of the garden was in the interest of preserving their peace. As the Creator, God knows us better than we do. But, then the first family lost their vision of God and His plan to keep them in perfect peace. They ate from the tree that God had forbidden them from eating and lost their peace for eternity.

Nothing in the world can rob you of your peace except sin. Every human being is designed to live in peace, but transgression takes away this privilege. As soon as the first family was sent out of the garden, they lost their peace. What this means is that there is no peace outside the garden (Genesis 2:15-17). There is no peace outside God. The sin of the first family and the penalty has been extended to every generation. And what that means is that every generation must seek God to undo what the first family did, because the standard of God is the same from generation to generation. But the good news is that God in His mercy came up with a recovery plan for the world to retain its peace. *"For unto us a child is born, unto us a son is given: and the government shall be upon his shoulder: and his name shall be called Wonderful, Counsellor, The mighty God, The everlasting Father, The Prince of Peace. Of the increase of his government and peace there shall be no end, upon the throne of David, and upon his kingdom, to order it, and to establish it with judgment and with justice from henceforth even forever. The zeal of the LORD of hosts will perform this"* (Isaiah 9:6-7). Note that the purpose of God sending His Son, the Prince of Peace, to the corrupt and sinful world is to set it in order with judgment and justice.

Until the issues of social injustice and power politics are addressed, there will be no peace in the world. The moment the first family lost their peace, the world was thrown into critical need for peace. H.G. Wells stated in his book, *New World Order* that a new world order was needed to unite the nations of the world to bring about peace and end war. Wells' new world order proposal includes establishing a legal institution that addresses human rights protection. For peace to reign in this world, there must be institutions that promote democracy and security. What we are witnessing in the world today is power politics and foreign policies that encourage international hostility.

When our wisdom and intellect fail us as humans, we must go back to God who gives wisdom liberally. There shall be no end to peace for any government that runs on the counsels and principles of God (judgment and justice). We must enthrone the culture of Judgment and justice at all levels of institutions to experience peace. When the first family traded their peace for sin (corruption) and the entire world was left without peace, God gave us the Prince of Peace to recover and lead the world into everlasting peace. When the world yields to Christ to lead the way, it will enjoy unending peace. It is written: *"These things I have spoken unto you, that in me ye might have peace. In the world ye shall have tribulation: but be of good cheer; I have overcome the world"* (John 16:33).

Living a life that models Christ brings peace, while pursuing worldly pleasures without regards for judgment and justice, on the other hand, leads to crisis and tribulation. The peace of God in you is able to drive you through situations and challenges of life. *"And the peace of God, which passeth all understanding, shall keep your hearts and minds through Christ Jesus"* (Philippians 4:7). We all walk through situations of varying degrees in this world, but only the peace of God can make us prevail over whatsoever challenges we face. The gift of peace is found in Jesus Christ. I am talking about the incomprehensible peace of God. This type of peace was what made Jesus remain calm even in the face of such cruel and shameful death, as being hanged on the cross like a common criminal for offences He did not commit, so that the world, through His dying, may live in eternal peace.

This act of Christ to sacrifice His life for the peace of others is beyond human understanding. Until we begin to make sacrifices and quit the "me and my family" syndrome, peace may continually be a mirage rather than a reality. When Christ finds you, He hands down His heritage of peace to you and you automatically become an instrument of peace. As a Kingdom's ambassador, the totality of your life's activities must promote peace.

It is comforting to know that the peace that God gives is that which surpasses all understanding (Philippians 4:7). Christ exemplified this peace that surpasses human understanding when He showed up in the stormy situation of Peter on the Sea of Galilee. The spectators of this unbelievable miracle could not understand the mystery. Jesus was seen walking on the Sea towards sinking Peter as he was beckoned by Christ to meet Him right in the middle of the Sea. The unspeakable happened when Peter contacted the peace in Christ and began to walk the bridgeless Sea towards Him.

Notice that peace is a precursor to miracle. I have seen this fact play out several times in my life. Whenever I write any exam, I try to get into the peace atmosphere, by inviting the presence of God in worship and in the end, the testimony is always beyond my comprehension. I have also heard stories of pregnant women who were told by their doctors their children were dead in their wombs, but ignored the doctors' report and upheld the report of the Lord in the atmosphere of peace and had their babies without complications. I also heard a story of a woman who lost her husband to an auto crash, but instead of wailing in hopelessness and despair, she tapped into the peace of God that surpasses human understanding. Instead of crying, she began to worship God contrary to the norm and contested the death of her husband at the court of heaven. In the end, her request was granted and her husband was brought to life by a simple prayer of an evangelist in a close by City Gospel Crusade.

Peace is the manifestation of the presence of God in human beings and it is the special gift for the saints. Are you living in perpetual crisis? Allow Christ into your heart and life, and you will begin to experience the peace of God beyond your wildest imagination.

CHAPTER FOUR

THE POSSIBILITIES OF PATIENCE

"Patience is a vibrant and virile Christian virtue, which is deeply rooted in the Christian's absolute confidence in the sovereignty of God and in God's promise to bring all things to completion in a way that most fully demonstrates His glory." —**Albert Mohler**

Patience is the ability to accept what you cannot change and change what you can, in order to achieve a definite goal in life. Oppositions and frustrations are strong adversaries of dreams and visions, but patience has strong wings that can bear you over them to the very place of utmost accomplishment. Joyce Meyer puts it this way: "Patient is the dark room where character is developed. There are numerous obstacles on our way to our destiny and purpose in life, but patience bears you on its wings to fly you over mountains of frustrations to the place you are meant to be." *"And not only so, but we glory in tribulations also: knowing that tribulation worketh patience; And patience, experience; and experience, hope"* (Romans 5:3-4).

It is important to realize that the devil uses tribulation to afflict humanity with frustration and when frustration sets in, the journey of purpose becomes impeded. The antidote to frustration is patience. Patience literally has a wing that bears you over all mountains and valleys of frustration. Patience simply means the ability to endure the pains of the present to ensure the gains of the future.

I have realized that, in life, you walk against the tides to arrive at your destination; and to overcome the tides, you need patience. Without patience you may not go far. Just reflect on Abraham, the father of faith; he embarked on a far journey of life and ended well because he exercised patience. It was at the age of ninety-nine that God started unfolding His purpose for Abraham, which was to make him the father of many nations. At this time, he had not borne Isaac, but Abraham remained patient and one year down the line, he had Isaac by his wife Sarah.

God has a specific purpose for every one of us

and tribulation cannot change His purpose for us. *"For I know the thoughts that I think toward you, saith the LORD, thoughts of peace, and not of evil, to give you an expected end"* (Jeremiah 29:11). Tribulation or failure is like a stop sign, but not the end of the journey. It is for you to stop for a minute and review your past, be in control of now and commit the future into God's hands. What puts you in charge of the now of your life is patience; because when we allow frustration to have a foothold on our lives, it brings about failure. Patience makes us move swiftly from failure to success.

Over the years, I have come to understand that some frustrations are deliberately built into the plans of God to keep us in His perfect will to take us to our peaceful purpose. Any deviation from the perfect will of God in an individual's life, has a generational implication. When Abraham yielded to the counsel of his wife to marry the Egyptian slave girl, it became a great conspiracy against the perfect will of God and the implication of that singular compromise is what we are seeing in our world today. *"And he will be a wild man; his hand will be against every man, and every man's hand against him; and he shall dwell in the presence of all his brethren"* (Genesis 16:12).

Patience gives you the emotional freedom that keeps you continuously in the perfect will of God to align you with your expected end of peace. Walking in the perfect plan of God for your life gives you a purposeful and peaceful end. The purpose of God for the world is to dwell in perfect peace, but look at where we are today, where is the peace? Impatience: the inability to wait for our time has turned our world into one of frustrations and failures.

Now, just like you have a specific time to move from one location to another, the journey of destiny is time-specific and it is only the wings of patience that will fly you there safely. A lot of people have ended their journeys before they reached their destination and lived the rest of their lives in perpetual struggling and sorrow. Just because you started at the same time with a friend does not mean that you are ending the same time; after all, even a set of twins that entered the world the same time do not necessarily end their lives the same day.

I know of people that ended up in a wrong career because of an assumption that they must end with a group they started with and lived in perpetual regret and emotional defeat for the rest of their lives. When you have to repeat a class and the rest of your friends are moving to the next class, it takes patience for you to see beyond that failure and move to the next level in your career. Patience takes you beyond the level of impulsive reasoning to that of intuitive reasoning where you will actually see rather than just looking. Yes, the fact that you are looking at something does not mean you are seeing it. But patience makes you relaxed and that enables you to see what you are looking at.

Jesus Christ was interrupted by the pains of the cross, but He was patient to see the gain and the joy of fulfilment that comes after the cross. *"Looking unto Jesus the author and finisher of our faith; who for the joy that was set before him endured the cross, despising the shame, and is set down at the right hand of the throne of God"* (Hebrews 12:2). Patience earns you acceptance and honor before God. The purpose of Christ is to mentor and model the world through a lifestyle that is acceptable by God. To be mentored and modeled by Christ, you will need to accept Him into your life, and you will begin to manifest patience as a life style. Patience is an evidence of the Spirit of God indwelling a man. Christ was patient enough to see right through the suffering on the cross to His purpose. He did not quit the process that led to His purpose, He rather endured the process to enjoy the proceeds.

Do not just keep looking at the process of your life's purpose; because if you do, you will lack the emotional strength to continue through to the proceeds. When you are traveling down the path of destiny, it is normal to experience different road bumps of frustrations, but patience offers you the resilience to see the joy that comes with the fulfilment of destiny. Many people have quit the journey of destiny because they lacked this precious and valuable gift of God through Christ and ended up achieving nothing. Each one of us is made to be something through something and until we go through something, we cannot be something. Going from something through something to the something of life requires diligence and resilience by patience.

God relates with us with patience and He expects us to keep this relationship through patience. No relationship exists without patience. Can you imagine friendship or marriage anywhere in the world without patience? A leader has to be patient to have followers and a teacher has to be patient to have students, and the list is inexhaustible. Nothing can be achieved under the sun without patience. Looking unto Jesus according to Hebrews 12:2 literally means making Christ your standard in your life's experiences to achieve your goals. The burden of the cross was not easy for him, but with patience, He stayed focused and made it through till He returned to the right hand of the Father. Success in life is a promise by God to the people, but only patience can translate it to success. "

For when God made promise to Abraham, because he could swear by no greater, he sware by himself, Saying, Surely blessing I will bless thee, and multiplying I will multiply thee. And so, after he had patiently endured, he obtained the promise" (Hebrews 6:13-15).

Abraham, the father of faith only received the promise of the free born through patience and endurance. When you surrender your life to Christ, He comes to dwell inside of you by faith and you will begin to bear the fruit of patience. One strong weapon against patience is anxiety. Anxiety makes you unstable and when you are unstable you lose focus and eventually quit. When you are born again, you pull off the garment of anxiety with your old nature and confidence in God begins to shape your character. To draw the attention of God, you must be confident in His words. *"If ye abide in me, and my words abide in you, ye shall ask what ye will, and it shall be done unto you"* (John 15:7). The word of God in you gives you confidence that translates into patience when you are going through the test of your life. At the time of trials, the devil targets the word of God in you to afflict your confidence level. When your confidence level in God drops, anxiety sets in to make you doubt God. Patience on the other hand makes you to tap into the power of the word to ensure victory beyond the trials.

I love to sing Roberts Greenlaw's patience song with my children. Here is the line that inspires me the most: "If you are patient, you will see your dream takes flight." He used this song to describe *patience* as the secret of transformative development that transforms the wingless ugly caterpillar to the beautiful winged butterfly.

You have to understand that for every dream to become a reality, the dreamer must be subjected to a cocoon experience. The essence of the cocoon to the life cycle of the butterfly is to ensure its safety as it goes through the developmental stages. We are all created with a protective cocoon and it takes patience to wait and be calm for this critical development seasons of life to pass in our lives. The cocoons of life sometimes appear like obstacles, but if you wait till the end of the obstacles, the miracles begin. The obstacles today work together for your miracles tomorrow. "And we know that all things work together for good to them that love God, to them who are the called according to his purpose" (Romans 8:28).

I believe that nobody is created for failure, except you fail the test of patience. Unlike the conventional test, which you can only take for a number of times, God allows us to attempt the test of patience until we pass. *"For a just man falleth seven times, and riseth up again: but the wicked shall fall into mischief"* (Proverbs 24:16). The righteousness imputed in you at salvation enlightens your understanding of spiritual warfare that patience in tribulation will give you victory in the end.

The battle of purpose cannot be won without patience. The wall that separates you and your purpose is impatience, because it makes you feel frustrated by situations and eventually pushes you to quit before arriving at your purpose. I can't remember any achievement in my life that was earned on the first attempt. You may be lucky to have earned all your achievements in life at the first attempt, depending on the circumstances that surrounded your birth or the environment in which you are brought up. If you are like me whose parents were both unbelievers, you will understand. I did not have the opportunity to know my father well enough before he died in 1975, when I was in first grade. He was a pagan and lacked the understanding of what it took to intercede for his children like Job. My father was a polygamist and if you came from a background like mine, you may have a little understanding of where I am coming from. The greatest hurt you can inflict on yourself in life is to be content with failure and resign to fate. Abraham Lincoln said and I quote. "My great concern is not whether you failed, but whether you are content with your failure." Real failure is failing to walk through failure until success is finally achieved.

The journey to purpose is full of spiritual resistance and patience will attract the presence of God to take over the fight. When patience brings God into your situation, He gives you the right word to overcome frustrations. Ruth could have remained a widow for life if she did not insist on sticking with Naomi, her mother-in-law. *"And Ruth said, Intreat me not to leave thee, or to return from following after thee: for whither thou goest, I will go; and where thou lodgest, I will lodge: thy people shall be my people, and thy God my God"* (Ruth 1:16). You must learn to speak to every wall of separation between you and your purpose.

Daniel made it clear to Nebuchadnezzar that he was ready to pay the price of death than to compromise his faith. While compromise takes you farther away from your purpose, patience hastens your purpose to appear. *"If it be so, our God whom we serve is able to deliver us from the burning fiery furnace, and he will deliver us out of thine hand, O king. But if not, be it known unto thee, O king, that we will not serve thy gods, nor worship the golden image which thou hast set up"* (Daniel 3:17-18). Daniel and his slave friends would have perished in Babylon and nothing would have been mentioned about them forever, but because they trusted in their God with patience, history will not forget them.

Esther also made a statement of faith while she patiently worked out her purpose. When a conspiracy mounted up against the collective purpose of her race, she took on the fight to the palace of the king with patience and faith in God for judgment and victory. In the end, Esther progressed from slavery to being a queen. *"Go, gather together all the Jews that are present in Shushan, and fast ye for me, and neither eat nor drink three days, night or day: I also and my maidens will fast likewise; and so will I go in unto the king, which is not according to the law: and if I perish, I perish"* (Esther 4:16). Always learn to say "no" to obstacles as you walk the path of destiny to avoid stopping half way.

Job, in his tribulation refused to give up, he patiently held unto God and his end was better than his beginning. *"For I know that my redeemer liveth, and that he shall stand at the latter day upon the earth: And though after my skin worms destroy this body, yet in my flesh shall I see God"* (Job 19:25-26).

Joseph was another man who with patience survived his own cocoon experience. His patience helped protect his dream through slavery and incarceration to becoming the second in command to Pharaoh in Egypt. When you wait on God in your affliction, God will make your afflicters to worship you. Notice that after Joseph was unlawfully sent to prison for protecting his God given dream, none of his afflicters had peace again. His brothers who sold him had to go and worship him to have food. After Joseph was sent to the prison for offences he did not commit by Potiphar, nothing was heard about him again and that was when Joseph began to see his dream take flight. The good thing about patience is that it produces fruits in tribulation. *And Joseph called the name of the firstborn Manasseh: For God, said he, hath made me forget all my toil, and all my father's house. And the name of the second called he Ephraim: For God hath caused me to be fruitful in the land of my affliction"* (Genesis 41:51-52).

The Spirit of God comes into the life of any who surrenders his life to Christ, and that one starts bearing fruits for human satisfaction and to the glory of God. Patience is one important component of the fruit of the Spirit that makes life worth living.

CHAPTER 5

THE BEAUTY OF GENTLENESS

"Gentleness has nothing to do with weakness, timidity, indifference, or cowardice. It was used of wild animals that were tamed, especially of horses that were broken and trained. Such an animal still has his strength and spirit, but its will is under the control of its master." —John MacArthur

Gentleness is a character trait inherited from God by the new birth through faith in Christ. And it manifests through tenderness and kindness. It is a character trait that is cherished by everyone because it is humble, generous, and respectful. Gentleness is the opposite of pride and arrogance. It is the ability to respect other people's feelings and values. It does not give up on being kind to people even when they're seemingly undeserving of kindness. Gentleness is the evidence of the presence of the Spirit of God in human beings because God never gave up on the world even when it was undeserving of His love, He gave His most priced and loved possession for the redemption of the world. God has since never given up on the world, despite its constant refusal and rebuttal of His love and ultimate sacrifice, He gives us His Holy Spirit, who is ever present to convict sinners of sin and provoke believers to righteousness.

The gentle nature of God was deposited in humanity from the time of creation but was corrupted and deactivated by sin and can only be reactivated by God's kindness or grace through faith in atoning work of Christ. *"For the grace of God that bringeth salvation hath appeared to all men, Teaching us that, denying ungodliness and worldly lusts, we should live soberly, righteously, and godly, in this present world; Looking for that blessed hope, and the glorious appearing of the great God and our Saviour Jesus Christ; Who gave himself for us, that he might redeem us from all iniquity, and purify unto himself a peculiar people, zealous of good works"* (Titus 2:11-14).

This Fruit of the Spirit, gentleness, like every other Fruit of the Spirit is brought on when the work of salvation is completed in an individual. At the point of salvation, the image of God is ignited to begin a fresh operation. To express the art of gentleness that is lasting and enduring, you must surrender to the Holy Spirit to bear this fruit. Jesus our perfect Example epitomized gentleness when on His way to Jerusalem, He passed by the city of Samarian and the inhabitants thereof were hostile to Him. He didn't repay their hostility with hostility, but remained kind to them. *And it came to pass, when the time was come that he should be received up, he stedfastly set his face to go to Jerusalem, And sent messengers before his face: and they went, and entered into a village of the Samaritans, to make ready for him. And they did not receive him, because his face was as though he would go to Jerusalem. And when his disciples James and John saw this, they said, Lord, wilt thou that we command fire to come down from heaven, and consume them, even as Elias did? But he turned, and rebuked them, and said, Ye know not what manner of spirit ye are of. For the Son of man is not come to destroy men's lives, but to save them. And they went to another village"* (Luke 9:51-56).

Jesus was kind to even His opposition and He expects nothing less than that from His followers. We are expected to be gentle to even our enemies to the extent of praying for them to be saved. We therefore have to be careful about what we pray about to avoid expending time and energy in praying amiss. If you claim to possess the gentle nature of God in Christ and you are praying for the destruction of people's lives, you may be in disconnect with God's will. Every prayer is said in Christ's name because He mediates between men and God, if therefore, your prayers are not in accordance with His purpose, they are going nowhere. John 14:12-13 says, *"Verily, verily, I say unto you, He that believeth on me, the works that I do shall he do also; and greater works than these shall he do; because I go unto my Father. And whatsoever ye shall ask in my name, that will I do, that the Father may be glorified in the Son."* If Christ was kind to His enemies, He expects us to be kinder to even greater enemies than He had. Except we come to this understanding, our communication channel with God will be blocked.

Moreover, the Fruit of kindness makes us to relate well with sinners to the intent of winning them over for Christ. Jesus Christ our model demonstrated kindness that accounted for huge success of His ministry within the short period of time He had on earth. He expressed this quality when the woman that was allegedly caught in adultery was brought before Him (See account in John 8:3-11).

To be an effective leader, you must bear this very important Fruit of the Spirit. Jesus knew that His purpose was to fulfil the law and make provision for a second chance (go and sin no more). I imagine that when He was looking and writing on the ground, He was saying in His mind that it was an opportunity for Him to let the accusers realize that His purpose was not to destroy lives but to save them. Instead of casting the first stone at your offenders in pride and self-righteousness, be gentle and offer a second chance. The Psalmist understood this, hence he said in psalm 130:3-4, *"If thou, LORD, shouldest mark iniquities, O Lord, who shall stand? But there is forgiveness with thee, that thou mayest be feared."* Apart from the fact that gentleness makes us great soul-winners and successful leaders, both spiritually and secularly, Jesus Christ declared in Matthew 5:5, *"Blessed are the meek: for they shall inherit the earth"*. Gentleness is key to fulfilling purpose in life.

We will now examine the critical areas of life for which gentleness is expedient to guarantee success.

GENTLENESS IN LEADERSHIP

It takes common sense to realize that there is no leadership without followership. A bullying manager will quickly lose his job, because in the end, he or she will have no one to manage. What makes good leadership is the ability to relate well with followers in the spirit of gentleness. Everyone wants to be loved and treated well, the absence of which results in strife and conflicts. The quickest way to grow your business as an employer is to be nice to your employees by respecting their feelings and rewarding performance. Gentleness earns you loyalty of your subjects as a leader, while pride and arrogance tear apart a kingdom.

Rehoboam, king of Judah lost his kingdom because he was not gentle to his subjects. *"And they spake unto him, saying, If thou wilt be a servant unto this people this day, and wilt serve them, and answer them, and speak good words to them, then they will be thy servants for ever"* (1 King 12:7). The words of the elders are the words of wisdom, they say, but Jeroboam rejected the gentle counsel of the elders and took the prideful and arrogant counsels of young people and finally got for himself a divided kingdom with only two of the twelve tribes of Israel under his control. When you are gentle as a leader, you bring out the potential in your subjects, but pride and arrogance diminishes and subdues interests.

GENTLENESS IN MARRIAGE

At the heart of every successful marriage is an attribute of the fruit of the Spirit called gentleness. I love to call it the wonder in marriage. Gloria and I had been married for fifteen years before I started writing this book. You wouldn't be holding this book right now were it not for gentleness. Both of us have made our marriage to be successful by gently embracing God to bless our marriage with the spirit of gentleness. We understood even before we came together that gentleness is an attribute of God and that He freely gives anyone that truly asks Him. When you are gentle, you will know gentleness when you see it.

The first time I found my wife, I saw the picture of gentleness on her face and waited until I was sure it was real before I made my intention known to her. The good thing with using the fruit of the Spirit to find a spouse is if you find one of the nine, others are there together because they are actually nine fruits encapsulated in one called the fruit of the Spirit. The special thing about this mystery is you must possess this fruit to find it. The fruit of gentleness gives you the conviction to identify the real one among the fake ones. When I met my wife, she was not well dressed. She was actually taking down her hair and looked very unappealing to the ordinary eyes. It was this fruit of gentleness that activated my patience (another fruit) to look beyond her appearance and I was able to see the substance of gentleness in her.

It is better to possess this fruit of the Spirit before you start looking for someone to get married to, because it will make your finding easy. It is like looking for what is branded as yours and you alone have the code to identify it. The code to identify your spouse *as* you *are* preparing for marriage is who you are.in essence, the understanding of who you are makes it easy to discover your spouse. It was very easy for Adam to find Eve because she possessed his brand of bone and flesh (Genesis 2:23). What gave Adam ability to identify his spouse was the express image of God in him.

Like Adam, we need the fruit of the Spirit (God's image) to identify our spouse, because the image of God in man left him when the body became corrupt by sin. Since the standard of God is the same across all generations, we need His image in us to dwell in His will and purpose which include marriage. For the image of God (Holy Spirit) to be relocated into our lives, therefore, we need to take-off the corrupt body and put on a new one through the new birth in Christ. *"Therefore if any man be in Christ, he is a new creature: old things are passed away; behold, all things are become new"* (2 Corinthians 5:17).

I interacted with many couples as I was writing this book and found that the secret of a successful marriage is knowing who your spouse is before looking for him or her for marriage. Abraham knew Isaac's wife and described her to his servant to get her for him. When you are walking in the Spirit of God, He gives you every detail to identify your spouse when you find him or her.

Gentleness is variously manifested in humility. Rick warren said humility is not thinking less of yourself but thinking of yourself less. Until you begin to think of yourself more than others, you will not serve others, which is the purpose of your creation. You must bring to the table, commitment to serve, to nurture your marriage. I have heard about relationships that broke because of who takes out the trash. As insignificant as this role may sound to you, it has caused a lot of broken relationships. If partners are bound together in relationship with the commitment to serve each other, none of the partners will ever see the trash full. You must understand that marriage relationship is complementary, and service to each other is the secret.

Once upon a time, I met Natasha and Arthur, who had been married for eight years at Hartsfield Atlanta International airport on their way from a vacation. My close observation of the couple suggested to me that they were committed to their relationship. Out of curiosity, I asked if they were married and they said yes. To me, eight years is a long time to be married and stay married to one spouse in the American society. Both Natasha and Arthur were in their early thirties, and for such people to have stayed together for this long, there certainly is commitment at the center.

I asked them to tell me one thing that has kept them together for the past eight years of their marriage with specific examples. Natasha was the first person that opened up and screamed "commitment"! She said that her husband had raised the bar of gentleness and commitment in their relationship, adding that when they took the decision for her to go back to school and be trained to be a nurse, Arthur was the one that was taking care of their four children, as well as running the home. When Arthur contributed to the discussion, he admitted that taking care of all four children, preparing their meals, doing the dishes after them and keeping the home, while Natasha was studying wasn't an easy task, but commitment kept him going.

Cultivating marriage relationship may not be an easy task, but gentleness and commitment makes it a lot easier.

Another factor that helps to tune-up relationship is gentleness in communication. A gentle spirit manifests in soft words. The Scripture says a soft word turns away wrath (Proverbs 15:1). Learn to communicate in a soft gentle spirit especially when your partner is tempted to raise his or her voice. Remember, gentleness is strength under control. One area that I think Gloria has done better than I in our relationship is in gentleness in communication. I learned from her how to overcome anger with soft words. Never raise your voice in response to your angry spouse, it will save you from many years of nursing a non-healing wound. Gentleness makes you know that you are not right all the times and your partner could be right some of the times. Gentleness is a mask that prevents you from seeing each other's weaknesses and faults. The scripture says; *"Be kindly affectioned one to another with brotherly love; in honour preferring one another"* (Romans 12:10). Be nice to your spouse in gifts and words, because you will earn his or her submission.

Just like Christ was gentle enough to have given Himself as an offering for sin, so that He could come into a relationship with His bride, the church, we must also be willing to give ourselves, indeed our all into relationship with our spouses. For a natural man, it is literally impossible to put everything you have in life into a relationship. Jesus Christ brought everything he had into his relationship with the church and that earned Him the submission of the church. The things you hold back from your marriage will take your attention from it. You must yield for Christ to come inside of you and He will make you submit to your relationship in the spirit of gentleness.

GENTLENESS IN PARENTING

Parenting is the process of promoting and supporting the physical, emotional, social and intellectual development of children from childhood to adulthood. Parenting is simply acting as a father or mother to someone; every child must be fathered or mothered by someone, regardless of whether you are available or not. Some parents are too busy to father or mother their children, thereby leaving this important role for strange parents. Parenting requires special knowledge and skill sets that are given by God to parents for their children's upbringing. The scripture says *Lo, children are an heritage of the LORD…"* (Psalm 127:3). Children are gifts from God to be mentored in a specific way, so that they can take their place in the world and bring about the fulfilment of God's plan and purpose for mankind.

It is worthy to note God who gave humans the responsibility of parenting has a blueprint which parents must follow in raising children who will fulfil their purpose in life. As parents, you must have a relationship with God to understand the way to train a child to become what God wants him or her to be. Anyone who does not have a relationship with God the giver of Children, does not and cannot understand God's design and pattern for child upbringing. This situation is even worse when the parents are of different faith because the child will grow up confused, or worse still, grow up without any principle in life. That is the reason why we have a lot of people not standing for something and consequently falling for everything.

Every child is a spirit being placed by God Himself

in an environment, for the purpose of managing that environment it in a manner that reflects the peace agenda of God for the world. The environment I am referring to is the totality of the parents and the ecological community the child is located. The first line of the environment is the parents in whose custody God has kept the child. Every parent has the responsibility of laying the foundation for the way the child should go in life and any fault at this level of parenting may be hard to correct at the community level.

Survey has shown that the best way of parenting is by living what we say than just giving instructions. Children are by nature imitators. They mostly do what they see their parents do, rather than what they hear them say. Most children I spoke to when I was writing this book stated that they believe in what they see their parents doing more than what they tell them to do. Parents are therefore required to balance instructions with actions for effective parenting. Actions, they say, speak louder than words.

Effective parenting begins with effective knowledge, which can only be received from the Giver of children. Parents must realize that God is the Giver of children and every information they need to raise them according to the purpose of the Giver is with Him, and He gives to those who acknowledge this and ask for them.

Gentleness is an especially important personality trait required to raise up children to align with the peace agenda of God. It takes gentleness to raise a child in a community where peace and tranquility reigns. Gentleness is an integral part of God's image that is acquired by those that are saved and are walking in the Spirit of God. Anyone who possesses this Fruit of the Spirit will not struggle with raising godly children, because he or she will effortlessly live a life of gentleness by yielding to the gentle Spirit within for parenting that reflects the glory of God. Paul said, *"I am crucified with Christ: nevertheless I live; yet not I, but Christ liveth in me: and the life which I now live in the flesh I live by the faith of the Son of God, who loved me, and gave himself for me"* (Galatians 2:20).

Remember you don't possess the trait of gentleness of your own and such cannot pass on to your children what you don't have. Studies have shown that effective parenting is to be as nice as a friend to your children. I know of a parent that said to me that he applied all methods he could think of to parenting his Son, but none yielded result until he decided to come down to the level of his son as a friend. Being a friend to your children is a very effective parenting skill, but by far more effective than befriending your children, is helping them make friends with Jesus, the friend of all. Yes, the best friend you can introduce to your children is Jesus Christ.

I personally think that nagging or raising one's voice to instruct children in parenting is wrong because by that approach, you may end up raising a bunch of rebels. I found out that raising one's voice in parenting subjects' children to accumulating grieves and hiding their feelings from their parents. This is a huge societal problem in 21st century parenting, because victims of such dysfunctional parenting will naturally seek for alternative parenting with either a total stranger or social media.

One important consideration in raising children with gentleness, in my opinion, lies in the saying, **"what goes around comes around."** The children you raise today will be the ones to take care of you tomorrow when you are old and need help. Imagine when a stranger raises your children because, you failed to pass your own values and heritage on to them owing to your lack of gentleness in getting along with them, you will definitely face a lot of strange attitudes from them when you need them in your old age. Imagine if you happen to be an organized person and your child was raised by strange parents who allowed everything go. And now that you are too old to keep your environment in order, but you have a child who takes pleasure in a cluttered room, you may die of emotional stress before your time.

One of the most challenging aspects of 21st century parenting is every parent must be able to answer questions asked by children. This is an extremely hard demand by most parents, because today's children are technology natives, making them smarter than their parents. To answer a question from someone that is smarter than you, you must be able to do a lot of homework in terms of making research, not from "google search" but from the Giver. *"If any of you lack wisdom, let him ask of God, that giveth to all men liberally, and upbraideth not; and it shall be given him"* (James 1:5). There is no doubt that there are no questions about life that have not been answered by God because He is all knowing (Omniscient), but google search is limited to human research.

What makes the difference in parenting is the Spirit of God indwelling in man which produces the ability to raise children with Godly heritage. I have a real life analysis of this fact. I did not grow up to really know my father because we lost him when I was about 6 years old. I understand that he did not have the opportunity to meet the Lord before he passed. I literally grew up without fatherly mentorship and I think this affected me in a way, but thank God, I met the Lord early in life. Here is my experience and analysis; the Spirit of God in the heart of men produces the fruit of gentleness that helps parents to mentor their children into successful adults.

I grew up and attended the same school with two of my childhood friends who are Medical doctors now, and by the grace of God, they were not better than me in class, but I realized the difference between us was, while both of their parents were good Christians, mine were not. When you raise godly children, the gentle nature of God in them attracts favor and helpers to connect them with their destinies and purposes. Gentleness develops a character that people would like to stick around with. It is impossible for one to parent children with a value that he or she does not possess because you can only give what you have. *"Be not deceived; God is not mocked: for whatsoever a man soweth, that shall he also reap"* (Galatians 6:7).

It is therefore impossible for you to be an alcoholic and raise children that are not alcoholics, because children do what they see you do, rather than what you tell them to do. Even as Godly people, we need to spend time with our children in parenting. Eli was a high priest but his two sons; Hophni and Phinehas were described as the children of Belial, the worst character assassination of the time (see account in 1 Samuel 2). It is not enough for one to possess godly heritage and expect to raise godly children without taking time to really teach them.

CHAPTER 6

THE EXCELLENCY OF GOODNESS

∞

"Goodness finds its fullest and highest expression in that which is willingly and sacrificially done for others. It is moral and spiritual excellence manifested in active kindness." —**Bruce Hurt**

Goodness is the quality and attribute of something or someone that is beneficial to others. It is the state of being morally good or sound. Goodness is a gesture (giving, serving…) motivated by love. God is good and everything about Him is good. No one can be good, except he or she is of God. *"And Jesus said unto him, Why callest thou me good? there is none good but one, that is, God"* (Mark 10:18). This scripture reveals that goodness

BEARING THE SPIRIT'S FRUIT

or the quality of being good is of God alone. What Jesus was actually saying to the self-righteous man in the above passage was that our self-righteousness or charitable activities do not necessarily amount to *goodness,* except we have a relationship with God through the New Birth experience.

Romans 8:16-17 reveals that *"The Spirit itself beareth witness with our spirit, that we are the children of God: And if children, then heirs; heirs of God, and joint-heirs with Christ; if so be that we suffer with him, that we may be also glorified together.* Goodness is the Fruit of the Spirit that represents the nature of God imputed to His adopted sons and daughters. Once you are saved, you begin to bear the fruit of goodness. Jesus Christ was addressed by the rich man as a good teacher, because he saw the fruit of goodness in Him.

Jesus Christ, however attributed the ability to produce good works to God alone. *"How God anointed Jesus of Nazareth with the Holy Ghost and with power: who went about doing good, and healing all that were oppressed of the devil; for God was with him"* (Acts 10:38). Producing good works in this world designed to oppose anything good requires the power of God to overcome opposing forces. Christ continued to do good until His death, regardless of oppositions, because the power of God was with Him. Therefore, goodness is actually the manifestation of the nature of God indwelling a believer in Christ.

100

The intention of God when He set out to create the world was to project His goodness, and this was evident in the way He moved upon the face of the earth in His might, working His creation wonders in every aspect of the world until He was fully satisfied that everything He made was good (Genesis 1:31). After the standard of the world was compromised through the fall of Adam and Eve, God sent His Son to restore it to its original state of goodness. *"Every good gift and every perfect gift is from above, and cometh down from the Father of lights, with whom is no variableness, neither shadow of turning. Of his own will begat he us with the word of truth, that we should be a kind of first fruits of his creatures"* (James 1:17-18).

To represent God in this dysfunctional world, we must produce good works, following the examples laid down by Jesus Christ. *"The Spirit of the Lord is upon me, because he hath anointed me to preach the gospel to the poor; he hath sent me to heal the brokenhearted, to preach deliverance to the captives, and recovering of sight to the blind, to set at liberty them that are bruised, To preach the acceptable year of the Lord"* (Luke 4:18-19). The Gospel of Jesus Christ was amazingly effective and widely accepted because it was packaged in *goodness.* For one to be an effective Kingdom gospel promoter, you must bear this important Spirit's fruit.

The gospel, as exemplified by Christ was in *doing,* not just *saying.* Scripture tells us that Jesus went about doing good, feeding the hungry, healing the sick, delivering those possessed by devils, and raising the dead. We must realize that the substance in the gospel is the *good news*. For instance, the good news is food for the hungry and freedom for the captives. Believers are the extension of God's Kingdom with the responsibility of packaging the gospel in *goodness* for ease of acceptability and spread across the world.

It took Christ only three and a half years to impact the whole world with this strategy. And He promised believers in John 14:12; *"Verily, verily, I say unto you, He that believeth on me, the works that I do shall he do also; and greater works than these shall he do; because I go unto my Father"* This is the challenging area for the present-day Christian faithful, because Christ already raised the bar too high, ordinarily speaking. It means, if Christ raised the dead and set the captives free, we are expected to out-perform Him in the light of this Scripture. Paul understood this mystery very well when he said *"I can do all things through Christ which strengtheneth me"* (Philippians 4:13).

The Scriptures cannot be broken and the Word of God is settled in heaven. *"God is not a man, that he should lie; neither the son of man, that he should repent: hath he said, and shall he not do it? or hath he spoken, and shall he not make it good?"* (Numbers 23:19). Jesus Christ gave us a mandate to continue impacting our communities with good works by using our wealth, professions, skills and talents, and He expects us to do better than Him because, knowledge has increased, making it easier to propagate the gospel in this dispensation than in His own dispensation.

When Jesus Christ was around on earth, doing good, healing the oppressed, binding the bruised and brokenhearted, raising the dead, propagating the gospel of salvation, the means of transportation was by foot, asses and donkeys, and water; communication was by word of mouth and letter writing. But now, God has blessed this generation with increased knowledge of technology which has made things a lot easier than they were during Jesus' sojourn here.

Increased research in transportation technology has resulted in the production of motor vehicles and airplanes, which provide better transportation services than what was obtainable during the time of Christ. Information Communication Technology (ICT) has also turned the world into a single community where distance is no longer a barrier to communication. We are now in the age where through social media and cable news, we can get any information from anywhere in the world, within seconds of events unfolding.

When I got the understanding of *"and greater works than this shall ye do"*, I started believing that I don't have any excuse for not manifesting this Fruit of the Spirit called goodness. I am told as a physician; you don't need to go to Africa to treat a patient there. You only need to correspond with a technician or a practice there. Imagine a physician in the United States of America or Australia treating a patient in Africa digitally. This is a fulfilment of *"and greater works than this shall ye do."*

Let us now look at a few examples of the good things that describe the Spirit's Fruit of Goodness as exemplified by Jesus Christ. They include forgiveness, healing the sick, feeding the hungry etc.

FORGIVENESS

The spirit of forgiveness is what gives our relationship with Christ a meaning. We are forgiven to forgive others. A forgiving spirit is what attracts God's attention to answer our prayers. Forgiveness was at the center of Christ's teaching about prayers. *"And forgive us our debts, as we forgive our debtors"*. (Matthew 6:12). Until death, Christ was addressing the importance of forgiveness to the extent that before His last breath, He prayed for His enemies. *"And when they were come to the place, which is called Calvary, there they crucified him, and the malefactors, one on the right hand, and the other on the left. Then said Jesus, Father, forgive them; for they know not what they do. And they parted his raiment and cast lots"* (Luke 23:33-34). The confirmation of true forgiveness is praying for your offenders as demonstrated by Christ at the point of death on the cross. It is therefore hard to believe that a Christian finds it hard to forgive, much less pray for his or her enemies. It does not logically add up for the Spirit of God to dwell inside of a person and he or she does not bear the Spirit's Fruit. Anyone that is genuinely saved should not struggle with forgiveness at all, because he or she is now lead by the Spirit of God with whom forgiveness is spontaneous.

During His ministry here on earth, Christ always addressed issues of significance with parables. The importance of forgiveness was clearly explained in the parable of the unmerciful servant as recorded in Matthew 18:31-35. The mercy of God produces forgiveness to shield sinners from His anger. It therefore means that without forgiveness, there is no salvation because salvation is the forgiveness of sins.

Forgiveness is supposed to be a lifestyle for Christians because salvation is earned through the forgiveness of sins. Anyone who does not forgive, does not deserve the mercy of God and so heaven is shot over such an individual. Since none of us is perfect on our own, we need to continually pay the bills of our imputed perfections by forgiving our offenders. We depend on the mercy of God every single day, and as soon as we stop forgiving our offenders, He withdraws His coverage of mercy from us. *"It is of the LORD'S mercies that we are not consumed, because his compassions fail not. They are new every morning: great is thy faithfulness"* (Lamentations 3:22-23).

To maintain continual relationship with God, believers must let go all accumulated offences because human relationship with God is based on forgiveness. The reason why you have an uninterrupted power supply in your home is because you pay the bills to your service provider, whenever you stop paying the bills, you lose the power supply. When a believer is no more living a lifestyle of forgiveness, he or she must have lost his or her salvation. If your existence depends on the forgiving mercy of God you must forgive your offenders.

"Then came Peter to him, and said, Lord, how oft shall my brother sin against me, and I forgive him? till seven times? Jesus saith unto him, I say not unto thee, Until seven times: but, Until seventy times seven" (Matthew 18:21-22). What Christ is literally teaching here is that, you need a continuous forgiveness, and that you don't deserve it if you don't forgive others.

HEALING

Healing is an evidence of the Spirit of God in the believer's life. *"And these signs shall follow them that believe;*

In my name shall they cast out devils; they shall speak with new tongues; They shall take up serpents; and if they drink any deadly thing, it shall not hurt them; they shall lay hands on the sick, and they shall recover" (Mark 16:17-18). The gospel is divinely designed to include healing for the sick. Divine healing does not require the skills of the believer, but faith in the word of God. It is important that a believer understands the healing power in the word and applies it to the healing process.

In the conventional curing process, the physician must have knowledge of medicine and apply it through examination, diagnosis, and prescription for curing to take place. The physician communicates the importance of a medication to the patient and persuades him or her to believe and agrees that he or she will use the medication as prescribed by the physician. In the divine healing process, however, both the sick and the believer who is going to pray for healing of the sick, have to agree in faith and believe in the healing power of prayers made in the name of Jesus.

The miracle word in conventional curing or divine healing is *agreement.* I remember when I was growing up as a young Christian on campus, I frequently took ill. The campus Physician was a Christian who always emphasized the difference between healing and curing. He said to me that if I believed on the medication, I was going to be cured, but if I believed in the healing power of God, I was going to be healed. My encounter with this Christian physician reinforced my faith in God and His healing power, and I chose healing over curing, because healing is permanent, while curing is temporal may rebound, and the difference between the two is faith in God over medication.

As believers commissioned by Christ for good works, we must learn from the disposition of this Christian physician towards the gospel. The question of self was not in the equation of his curing and healing methodology. When you remove yourself and replace God in the equation of your success in life, you will be outstanding. I went out from the campus clinic that fateful day with a mind-blowing understanding that has helped me in my Christian journey. I realized then, that while emotional persuasion can cure, spiritual conviction heals. You may learn and possess emotional skills to persuade an audience, but spiritual conviction can only manifest as the Fruit of the Holy Spirit in those that possess the Spirit of God. The difference between a physician who administers healing and that which administers cure is that the healing physician possesses the Spirit of God in addition to acquired curative skills.

As believers, let us take ourselves from the picture of healing and let God in and we will be amazed by the magnitude of miracles that will occur in our ministries. There is no healing miracle without faith in God. *"And the prayer of faith shall save the sick, and the Lord shall raise him up; and if he have committed sins, they shall be forgiven him"* (James 5:15).

FEEDING THE HUNGRY

This is the most effective method ever used to convey the gospel in the history of Christianity. There is a growing spiritual and physical hunger ravaging the world. Jesus our perfect example addressed these two problems from the physical to the spiritual. The physical being determines what is fed to the spirit being; *"And the spirits of the prophets are subject to the prophets"* (1 Corinthians 14:32).

It is impossible to have spiritual transformation without emotional transformation. The door to spiritual transformation is the feeling and the emotion of the physical being and it takes compassion to open it. Most of the nations that are peaceful due to the patriotic spirit of the citizens have different welfare programs that address hunger and poverty. Shabina S. Khatri: an American freelance journalist once tweeted in THE WORLD POST that protest will not happen in Qatar because the government has laudable welfare programs that care for the basic needs of its citizens.

Jesus Christ was made manifest to usher in peace

into the world. He was introduced by Prophet Isaiah as the Prince of Peace. He understood the way of ensuring community peace, so much that Christ persuaded Peter to feed His sheep to prove his love for Him.

Notice that Jesus as the Prince of Peace carries the DNA of peace. Prince means a son of the king; it then follows that Christ is the son of Peace whose passion and purpose is to implement the peace program of God on earth. At the beginning of Peters' ministry, Jesus counseled him that if he really wanted to be successful, he needed the loyalty and attention of people and the only way to achieve that was to feed the people. *"So, when they had dined, Jesus saith to Simon Peter, Simon, son of Jonas, lovest thou me more than these? He saith unto him, Yea, Lord; thou knowest that I love thee. He saith unto him, Feed my lambs"* (John 21:15).

When Peter started applying the feeding the hungry method to the Gospel, his church began to experience an exponential growth. Feeding the hungry method of the gospel makes believers to connect to the spiritual being by addressing physical needs. *"And they, continuing daily with one accord in the temple, and breaking bread from house to house, did eat their meat with gladness and singleness of heart, Praising God, and having favour with all the people. And the Lord added to the church daily such as should be saved"* (Acts 2:46-47). To receive the favor of God for personal and ministerial increase, we must address both the physical and the spiritual needs of our audience. Jesus Christ first of fall fed the five thousand, and after getting their attention, He introduced Himself as the bread of life. We must follow the pattern of Jesus to make meaningful impact in the lives of people.

We are obligated to impact lives with the good news, and if we fail in this important divine responsibility, we will be held accountable. *"Then shall the King say unto them on his right hand, Come, ye blessed of my Father, inherit the kingdom prepared for you from the foundation of the world: For I was an hungred, and ye gave me meat: I was thirsty, and ye gave me drink: I was a stranger, and ye took me in: Naked, and ye clothed me: I was sick, and ye visited me: I was in prison, and ye came unto me. Then shall the righteous answer him, saying, Lord, when saw we thee an hungred, and fed thee? or thirsty, and gave thee drink? When saw we thee a stranger, and took thee in? or naked, and clothed thee? Or when saw we thee sick, or in prison, and came unto thee? And the King shall answer and say unto them, Verily I say unto you, Inasmuch as ye have done it unto one of the least of these my brethren, ye have done it unto me"* (Matthew 25:34-40).

Those who put the knowledge of God into work or programs to benefit those in needs are described as the righteous by King Jesus according to these Scriptures. Righteousness is the nature of God

111

imputed in believers at the point of salvation. *The logic in this scenario is that the righteousness of God imputed in believers is an investment that is expected to yield returns beneficial to humanity. It is clear from the judgment of the king that righteousness translates into good works and if anyone claims to be saved, he or she is expected to be a reflection of righteousness by bearing this Fruit of the Spirit called goodness. "And therefore it was imputed to him for righteousness. Now it was not written for his sake alone, that it was imputed to him; But for us also, to whom it shall be imputed, if we believe on him that raised up Jesus our Lord from the dead; Who was delivered for our offences, and was raised again for our justification"* (Romans 4:22-25).

From the teaching of Christ in this parable, He made it very clear that feeding the hungry is one of the important components of God's welfare program for the world *(For I was an hungred, and ye gave me meat)*. If we must be successful in the master's business, we must apply his method. As believers, we are on a journey that requires accountability like the narratives in this teaching of Christ. I have learned from my life's experience that a journey is made easier and reasonable with the end in mind and the outcome of every journey is determined from the beginning.

Here, we are told that to end well and be welcomed into the Kingdom prepared for the righteous from the foundation of the world, we must possess the righteousness of God through salvation and put our righteousness into good works to benefit those in need. The shocking understanding, I am getting from this teaching is that salvation is not equivalent to righteousness, it just places you in a better position to attain righteousness. The fieriest information to all of us who are inactive and remain at our comfort zones is that nothing at all was mentioned about Christians or believers in relation to righteousness.

The Scriptures say that all nations shall gather before the King (Jesus), and He shall separate the sheep (righteous) from the goats (unrighteous). It means that both the saved and sinners alike will be in the same crowd before the soon coming King, waiting for their judgment verdict. The judgment of this coming King will not be about whether you are the best preacher or the best church worker, neither will it be about whether you are of one religion or the other, it is going to be about how you put the knowledge of God in you (imputed righteousness) into good works.

We were told in the past that salvation gives the ticket to heaven; yes, frankly speaking, but you must show your good works to justify the validity of your ticket at the time of boarding the flight. If salvation is valid regardless of how we handle it, Paul could have not encouraged the Philippians to work out their salvation with fear and trembling. *"Wherefore, my beloved, as ye have always obeyed, not as in my presence only, but now much more in my absence, work out your own salvation with fear and trembling"* (Philippians 2:12). A Christian without the visible evidence of the Spirit's fruit denies the gospel of Jesus Christ and will be denied by Him in the end. *"But whosoever shall deny me before men, him will I also deny before my Father which is in heaven"* (Matthew 10:33).

It is important to realize that justification is by faith, perfected in good works, because faith without work is dead. *"What doth it profit, my brethren, though a man say he hath faith, and have not works? can faith save him? If a brother or sister be naked, and destitute of daily food, And one of you say unto them, Depart in peace, be ye warmed and filled; notwithstanding ye give them not those things which are needful to the body; what doth it profit? Even so faith, if it hath not works, is dead, being alone Yea, a man may say, Thou hast faith, and I have works: shew me thy faith without thy works, and I will shew thee my faith by my works. Thou believest that there is one God; thou doest well: the devils also believe, and tremble. But wilt thou know, O vain man, that faith without works is dead? Was not Abraham our father justified by works, when he had offered Isaac his son upon the altar? Seest thou how faith wrought with his works, and by works was faith made perfect? And the scripture was fulfilled which saith, Abraham believed God, and it was imputed unto him for righteousness: and he was called the Friend of God. Ye see then how that by works a man is justified, and not by faith only. Likewise also was not Rahab the harlot justified by works, when she had received the messengers, and had sent them out another way? For as the body without the spirit is dead, so faith without works is dead also"* (James 2:14-26).

CHAPTER 7

THE SHIELD OF FAITH

"Faith is a living, daring confidence in God's grace, so sure and certain that a man could stake his life on it a thousand times." —**Martin Luther**

Faith is an absolute trust or confidence in something. It is the religious doctrine that promotes strong belief in the existence of God, based on spiritual conviction rather than proof. Faith is believing that there is an invisible beyond the visible; for instance, the world and all it contains is the visible and beyond it is the invisible (God). Faith is the ability to see beyond the visible evidence or facts. Believers must understand that

117

faith is the direct opposite of facts. While faith is based on revelation, fact is based on investigation.

One of the scenarios that shows the difference between faith and fact was the meeting of Christ with His twelve disciples after His resurrection. One of the disciples of Jesus whose name was Thomas was told of the resurrection of Christ, but he demanded to see the specific evidence of the wounds inflicted on his Master before he could believe. *"But Thomas, one of the twelve, called Didymus, was not with them when Jesus came. The other disciples therefore said unto him, We have seen the Lord. But he said unto them, Except I shall see in his hands the print of the nails, and put my finger into the print of the nails, and thrust my hand into his side, I will not believe"* (John 20:24-25). Thomas was a fact-driven person and could only believe by seeing the evidence, a factor that I personally refer to as a spiritual disability, because he lacked the power to see beyond the visible.

A faith-driven person on the other hand believes in the substance behind the evidence (which is the invisible) through revelation by the knowledge of the invisible God. *"But without faith it is impossible to please him: for he that cometh to God must believe that he is, and that he is a rewarder of them that diligently seek him"* (Hebrews 11:6). To relate with God, you must believe in His existence before the evidence of His existence can be visible to you. Because God is a Spirit, He can only be visible to you when you operate in the Spirit through confidence in the knowledge of His word.

The presence of God in the heart of man can direct him in the path of seeing and understanding the invisible power of God. In other words, faith is the evidence of the presence of the Spirit of God in a believer, hence a Fruit of the Spirit. *"So then faith cometh by hearing, and hearing by the word of God"* (Romans 10:17). Faith is therefore the ability to hear God speak through His word and the assurance of His power therein.

Now, let us explore the concept of faith from the perspective of the Epistle to the Hebrews. The epistle to the Hebrews opens with clear definition of what faith is. *"Now faith is the substance of things hoped for, the evidence of things not seen"* (Hebrews 11:1).

A substance is defined as the real physical matter of which a person or thing consists, and which has tangible, solid presence. It is also safe to say that substance means the reality of existence. Faith is, therefore, the power that reveals the knowledge of the existence of unseen realities. *"Through faith also Sara herself received strength to conceive seed, and was delivered of a child when she was past age, because she judged him faithful who had promised. Therefore sprang there even of one, and him as good as dead, so many as the stars of the sky in multitude, and as the sand which is by the sea shore innumerable"* (Hebrews 11:11-12). While faith sees beyond the seen evidence to the unseen substance, fact only stops at the seen evidence.

Evidently, Abraham was barren, but by faith he was a substantial father of many nations. Faith is an equivocal trust in God to perform His word. By faith Daniel and his Hebrew friends were able to defend their belief in God before the Babylonian dictator, Nebuchadnezzar, by refusing to worship the king's god. *"Shadrach, Meshach, and Abednego, answered and said to the king, O Nebuchadnezzar, we are not careful to answer thee in this matter. If it be so, our God whom we serve is able to deliver us from the burning fiery furnace, and he will deliver us out of thine hand, O king. But if not, be it known unto thee, O king, that we will not serve thy gods, nor worship the golden image which thou hast set up"* (Daniel 3:16-18). When you challenge God with faith that is indifferent to situations, he becomes your defense. The three Hebrew children were taken in slavery; a situation where they were stripped off their rights to defend their belief. These believers had attained the level of faith that could not be intimidated by the king's repeated threats of death sentence by burning.

Faith is the substance that translates situations into testimonies of the reality of God's presence. *"Then Nebuchadnezzar the king was astonied, and rose up in haste, and spake, and said unto his counsellors, Did not we cast three men bound into the midst of the fire? They answered and said unto the king, True, O king. He answered and said, Lo, I see four men loose, walking in the midst of the fire, and they have no hurt; and the form of the fourth is like the Son of God"* (Daniel 3:24-25). Daniel and his slave friends heard the king's intimidating decrees but chose to act on the divine instructions of the almighty God. The substance of faith is the ability to tenaciously hold onto God through situations.

David also demonstrated the substance of faith by speaking to his situations; *"Yea, though I walk through the valley of the shadow of death, I will fear no evil: for thou art with me; thy rod and thy staff they comfort me"* (Psalm 23:4). Substantial faith is ignoring the fear of shadows and speaking out the reality. While fear shuts your mouth in the face of trials, faith keeps you vocal to claim your victory. Hannah was not muted by her situation of barrenness, she intentionally spoke to her situation to bring forth the substance of her faith, which came in the form of a male child, Samuel (See account in 1 Samuel 1:1-20).

Every one of us has an unseen godly heritage, and it is only by faith we can call it into existence for us to possess. Sometimes, life's situation masks the substance of faith from us and it takes the power of the word and faith to unmask those substances. For Hannah, she presented her petition through crying. Hannah's method of getting back her invisible heritage has worked for me several times in my faith walk. Let me share my experience of how I applied Hannah's method to get back my heritage from unseen enemies that attempted to rob me recently. As a member of the Redeemed Christian Church of God, I decided to take my situation to one of the annual conventions of the Church in North America. I was connected to a servant of God who was a fervent believer of Hannah's method. He suggested to me to come praying and fasting each day to the convention. At the end of the convention he came to my hotel room and agreed with me for total recovery of my stolen heritage and we left.

Alone in my hotel room, during the period of the convention, I poured out my sorrows in tears to God for the recovery of my stolen heritage. When I got home after the convention, I held the hands of my wife in prayers to jointly endorse my agreement with the servant of God at the convention (Hannah's Shiloh). About two minutes into our prayers, the phone rang and I was persuaded to pick it and lo and behold, I was reinstated and compensated. The substance of faith is revealed by speaking the words of faith to the situations holding back the manifestations of our heritage and testimonies.

The substance of faith is hope in hopeless situations. Ezekiel saw a hopeless and lifeless valley of dry bones, but God persuaded him to speak the words of faith to the bones and hope for the substance in the bones (the great army). *"Again he said unto me, Prophesy upon these bones, and say unto them, O ye dry bones, hear the word of the LORD. Thus saith the Lord GOD unto these bones; Behold, I will cause breath to enter into you, and ye shall live: And I will lay sinews upon you, and will bring up flesh upon you, and cover you with skin, and put breath in you, and ye shall live; and ye shall know that I am the LORD. So I prophesied as I was commanded: and as I prophesied, there was a noise, and behold a shaking, and the bones came together, bone to his bone. And when I beheld, lo, the sinews and the flesh came up upon them, and the skin covered them above: but there was no breath in them. Then said he unto me, Prophesy unto the wind, prophesy, son of man, and say to the wind, Thus saith the Lord GOD; Come from the four winds, O breath, and breathe upon these slain, that they may live. So I prophesied as he commanded me, and the breath came into them, and they lived, and stood up upon their feet, an exceeding great army"* (Ezekiel 37:4-10).

The great army (substance) in the seemingly dry bones could not be seen by Ezekiel until he began to speak to the hopeless situation to uncover the substance inside of the dry bones. Your spoken word of faith has the potential to uncover your hidden testimonies. I am a living witness to the miracle of speaking to a hopeless situation to bring out the substance of faith. My spiritual leader and the senior pastor of my church taught me how to go for the substance of faith in hopeless situations.

Many years ago, he sent me to go and speak to a situation like Ezekiel's dry bones experience.

My assignment was to speak to a lifeless pre-term baby at Emory hospital in Atlanta Georgia, USA. When I arrived at the Children Ward, it was obvious that everybody including the care team was waiting for the uncommon miracle. At this moment, the picture of the valley of dry bones came to mind and I began to speak to the situation holding back the baby from starting the journey of purpose, after the prayer, I left. Some weeks later, the baby was brought to our church to be dedicated. The family of this miracle baby relocated and no longer attend our church, but every year they bring the child to our annual festival of worship as a substance of faith and testimony.

Finally, brethren, the substance of faith is the unseen evidence revealed after faith has been correctly applied to situations by acting strictly on the instructions of the indwelling power of God (Holy Spirit) in a believer. Hence faith is evidently a Fruit of the Spirit of God.

CHAPTER 8

THE TRIUMPH OF TEMPERANCE

"A temperate man doesn't lose his physical, psychological and spiritual orientation. He is stable and steadfast, and his thinking is clear."
—**Gene Getz**

The word temperance can also be translated to mean self-control. This is the ability to do all things in moderation. It is the manifestation of the Spirit of God in a believer through the fruit of the Spirit. Self-control enables believers to live a life that is void of sin and resistant to temptations. It is the ability to identify sources of sin and temptation and avoid them. In 1 Thessalonians 5:22, Apostle Paul admonished the Thessalonian believers to *"Abstain from all appearance of evil."*

Temperance is the ability to apply the word of God correctly to life's situations in accordance with His will and purpose. The power to be temperate comes from the Spirit of God inputted in man, because of salvation and sanctification. A believer that can identify sin (esteeming the desires of the flesh over that of the spirit) and avoid it is manifesting Temperance as a Fruit of the Spirit. Temperance is the ability to yield to the voice and will of God over personal ambitions. *"This I say then, Walk in the Spirit, and ye shall not fulfil the lust of the flesh. For the flesh lusteth against the Spirit, and the Spirit against the flesh: and these are contrary the one to the other: so that ye cannot do the things that ye would"* (Galatians 5:16-17).

Your daily decisions and actions are informed of the spirit that rules your life. A life that is not ruled by the Spirit of God will manifest the desires of the flesh (sin) which is contrary to that of God's Spirit (righteousness). *"It is written; Now the works of the flesh are manifest, which are these; Adultery, fornication, uncleanness, lasciviousness, Idolatry, witchcraft, hatred, variance, emulations, wrath, strife, seditions, heresies, Envyings, murders, drunkenness, revellings, and such like: of the which I tell you before, as I have also told you in time past, that they which do such things shall not inherit the kingdom of God"* (Galatians 5:19-21). Temperance affords a believer the lifestyle that overcomes temptations and gives him power to live above sin. Let us examine few ways that temperance or self-control shapes an individual's life for victorious living.

TEMPERANCE AND TEMPTATION

Temperance is the ability to control self and stand at the time of trials and temptations. This is a divine ability given by God to those who harbor His spirit. "Ye have heard that it was said by them of old time, Thou shalt not commit adultery: But I say unto you, That whosoever looketh on a woman to lust after her hath committed adultery with her already in his heart. And if thy right eye offend thee, pluck it out, and cast it from thee: for it is profitable for thee that one of thy members should perish, and not that thy whole body should be cast into hell. And if thy right hand offend thee, cut it off, and cast it from thee: for it is profitable for thee that one of thy members should perish, and not that thy whole body should be cast into hell" (Matthew 5:27-28). The fruit of the Spirit that guarantees the believers freedom from sin is self-control or temperance.

As a teenage Christian, I used to believe I could sleep on the same bed with a female without having sex, until a day came that I had an experience but could not even sleep. There was a struggle between my spirit and the flesh that kept me awake. There is a difference between having the mental knowledge of self-control and bearing it as the Spirit's fruit. A tree should have no struggle with bearing fruits because it is supplied with the necessary nutrients it requires to bear fruits. What played out in my experience was an evidence that I did not have a good understanding of self-control as the Fruit of the Holy Spirit.

Self-control gives you an opportunity to avoid temptation before you are entangled. Jesus Christ demonstrated this Fruit of the Spirit when the devil challenged His faith. *"Then the devil taketh him up into the holy city, and setteth him on a pinnacle of the temple, And saith unto him, If thou be the Son of God, cast thyself down: for it is written, He shall give his angels charge concerning thee: and in their hands they shall bear thee up, lest at any time thou dash thy foot against a stone. Jesus said unto him, It is written again, Thou shalt not tempt the Lord thy God"* (Matthew 4:5-7).

Temperance or self-control as a Fruit of the Holy Spirit helps an individual identify and avoid sources of temptation and what the temptation may lead to. I did not understand when a pastor was forbidding his members from watching television. The way it was understood by his followers including me at that time was that, it was an intentional sin to watch television. Many of us struggled with this teaching for a long time, because for us at that time, there was no life without the television. When I was growing up in Africa, there were television programs we looked forward to; the blends of the "Cock crow at dawn", "Samanja", "Papa Ajasco" "Behind the scene" and so on. You will look stupid to meet your friends with nothing to discuss from the previous night's edition of the trending television programs. Some of us could not stay away from watching soccer, because it was part of life. So, I continued to struggle with this teaching until I received the revelation that gave me the full understanding of the Fruit of the Holy Spirit.

The pastor was interested in making his followers understand the essence of avoiding temptation, because it may be difficult for one to rebound. To thrive in this Christian journey, you must understand, possess, and bear the Spirit's Fruit. Satan, who tempted Christ and failed is very much around today to tempt and lure believers into sin. The devil failed in the case of Christ because He possessed the knowledge and the power of the Holy Spirit. Like Christ you must be able to identify every form of temptation and avoid them because prevention is better than cure.

Jesus understood the danger of temptation in the life of believers when He spoke about it while teaching His disciples about prayer. *"And lead us not into temptation, but deliver us from evil: For thine is the kingdom, and the power, and the glory, for ever. Amen"* (Matthew 6:13). If Jesus taught us to pray against temptation,

129

then we should endeavor to avoid it altogether. And to be sensitive to and avoid temptations, the believer needs self-control.

Satan uses temptations to challenge the believer's faith and testimony of salvation. Temptation leads to sin and since God requires the believers to be holy as He is (1 Peter 3:15-16) the devil will stop at nothing to make the believer yield to temptation to sin. Eve was tempted of the devil to sin and many generations after, we are still reaping the suffering that resulted in her yielding to temptation. Satan is still in the business of looking for whom to destroy with his subtle deceit and crafty temptation. Today, there is an increasing need for believers to seek to have this Fruit of the Spirit called temperance to enable them to identify and avoid temptations and their sources.

Truly, increase in knowledge in this dispensation has also widened the scope of temptation that is sweeping a lot of saints from faith. This will take us back to critically look at the teaching of the spiritual leader I mentioned earlier. Television is one of the oldest media technologies in the history of man that has been an all-time household companion. Honestly if you view most of the television programs and advertisement with the eyes of the Spirit, you will realize that they are designed for tempting the saints to sin. An unsanctified believer will find it difficult to manage temptations associated with television programs and advertisements, especially those related to sex and nudity. A Spirit-filled believer on the other hand will be able to select what is spiritually healthy to watch. It is even worse now that everybody can watch all sorts of things on mobile devices resulting in proliferated sources of temptations and astronomical increase in sins.

Most addictions to sinful lifestyles are acquired from television programs and related social media technologies. We are living in the world where it is literally impossible to do anything without the use of technology, we need this unique fruit of the spirit called **Temperance or self-control** to maintain spiritual integrity. I recall switching on my computer at work some time ago, and a lot of things popped up on the screen, which images lingered on my mind for a while. Most of the things I used to watch on television, I now consider as things that are injurious to the Spirit. It takes common sense to know that what goes in must come out. It is written. *"Be not deceived; God is not mocked: for whatsoever a man soweth, that shall he also reap"* (Galatians 6:7).

TEMPERANCE AND LEADERSHIP

Temperance is recommended for good and successful leadership in every sphere of life; from running a home to managing a public institution, you cannot overemphasize the indispensability of this Fruit of the Holy Spirit. *"So then it is not of him that willeth, nor of him that runneth, but of God that sheweth mercy"* (Romans 9:16). Good and successful leadership is given by God and it is manifested in those His Spirit indwells. Jesus was a good and successful leader because the Spirit of God was upon Him. *"The Spirit of the Lord is upon me, because he hath anointed me to preach the gospel to the poor; he hath sent me to heal the brokenhearted, to preach deliverance to the captives, and recovering of sight to the blind, to set at liberty them that are bruised, To preach the acceptable year of the Lord"* (Luke 4: 18-19).

Every leader is given specific leadership mandates and it takes self-control to shield him from anything capable of distracting him from accomplishing those leadership mandates. Moreover, a true leader is confronted with expectations either from statutory regulations, subordinates or contemporaries, and temperance is what makes him realize that he does not know it all and that his opinion may not always be the best. Temperance makes a good leader gracefully take responsibility for failure of the organization and willingly attribute success to his team. I like the way Arnold A. Glasow puts it; *"A good leader takes a little more than his share of the blame, a little less than his share of the credit."*

132

When a leader allows his personal ego to edge out God from his leadership equation, the result becomes failure. One thing that I have learned from my spiritual leader is "leading from behind." He so much manifests self-control as Fruit of the Spirit that he leads his team from behind, so much that if you are a guest in his congregation, you will not know who the leader is. It was Nelson Mandela, who said, **"It is better to lead from behind and to put others in front, especially when you celebrate victory when nice things occur. You take the front line when there is danger. Then people will appreciate your leadership."**

TEMPERANCE IN PARENTING AND MENTORING

In parenting and mentoring, actions are louder and more effective than words. Children and the mentored learn faster from actions than instructions. Temperance or self-control is the nature of God in parents and mentors, which make them to come to that place where the art of parenting and mentoring become result oriented. James Baldwin once said that **"Children have never been very good at listening to their elders, but they have never failed to imitate them."**

You must be conscious of your actions as parents or mentors because many have ruined their children or mentored by acting in the direct opposite of their words. David was given to sexual promiscuity, and that inability to control his sexual urge was replicated in Amnon his son. *"And she answered him, Nay, my brother, do not force me; for no such thing ought to be done in Israel: do not thou this folly. And I, whither shall I cause my shame to go? and as for thee, thou shalt be as one of the fools in Israel. Now therefore, I pray thee, speak unto the king; for he will not withhold me from thee. Howbeit he would not hearken unto her voice: but, being stronger than she, forced her, and lay with her. Then Amnon hated her exceedingly; so that the hatred wherewith he hated her was greater than the love wherewith he had loved her. And Amnon said unto her, Arise, be gone"* (2 Samuel 13:12-15).

It impossible to offer what you do not possess; Amnon was not better than a fornicator, because, the sin ran in their family and required temperance or self-control to undo it. As parents and mentors, you must be conscious of your actions and inactions, because learning is faster to the children through parental actions and inactions. The purpose of procreation is to ensure the continuous existence and management of the world. It is therefore the responsibility of the parents to pass-on the skills acquired from their parents to their children to manage and take charge of their domains.

Anyone that fails in his or her parenting has failed a divine responsibility. It is written; *"But if any provide not for his own, and specially for those of his own house, he hath denied the faith, and is worse than an infidel"* (1 Timothy 5:8). The word "provide" means to make available that which is needed to make lives worth living. When you are entrusted with children (the goodly heritage), it becomes your responsibility to provide them the skills that will develop them into responsible adults to manage a responsible community. It takes a responsible parent to raise a responsible community. A dysfunctional family will produce a dysfunctional child as well as a dysfunctional community where crisis and impunity will thrive against the divine will and purpose of God for the world.

The importance of self-control in parenting and mentoring cannot be over emphasized because you will be accountable as a parent or a mentor. This is important because you must realize what provision is needed for the child at a certain state of his or her development. Your parenting skills should reflect areas such as your tone in communication. **"YELLING silences your message. Speak quietly, so your children can hear your words instead of just your voice". —L.R. Knost.**

According to a research finding published in the Journal of marriage and family; families with 25 or more yelling incidents in 12 months, children can end up with lowered self-esteem, an increase aggression toward others and higher rates of depression. A teacher in the community where I live once call a parent and stated that the child always yells when communicating with mates and asked if anything was wrong with the method of communication at home. This was not a good day for those parents. It sounds to me that the teacher was conducting an assessment for possible diagnosis of verbal and emotional abuse.

Journal of Child Development (2014) reported that yelling at your kids can be just as bad as corporal punishment and it could cause behavioral problems and emotional development issues. Children who are always screamed at live with the perception of themselves as insignificant humans without the abilities to contribute to the development of their communities. The GOODVIBE.CO stated that "If you learn self-control, you can master anything". In every walk of life, self-control is to unlock the potential for success. From running a home to corporate institution or government office, self-control is key. Your public image is largely dependent on whether you possess this Fruit of the Spirit or not.

A leader that possesses self-control or temperance enjoys loyalty of followership, because it helps to moderate causes and effects of every decision. A self-controlled life is moderation driven; evident in living within ones means. When you are spending more than your income, you need a tune up in the spirit because, you are heading towards financial distress and failure with lack of self-control the root cause. Self-control also has been identified as the factor that helps to fortify marriage vows. A believer who is spirit-filled, will never give up on the marriage vows (for better, for worse), no matter tough the experience may be.

As a realist, there are many reasons to give-up on the marriage vows, but a self-controlled driven life sees those as associated cost of relationship. A self-controlled life always evaluates problems objectively, without being too quick to apportion blames to others, he or she accepts faults and show remorse for such actions. Another important evidence of self-controlled life is forgiveness, a very essential factor in relationship. Notice that self-control is an evidence of the presence of God (Holy Spirit) in the life of a believer whose nature is love and forgiveness.

When you have a believer, who claims to be Spirit-filled and he or she is talking about second and third marriage that has nothing to do with death of partners, it does not simply add up. It is written; *"Howbeit when he, the Spirit of truth, is come, he will guide you into all truth: for he shall not speak of himself; but whatsoever he shall hear, that shall he speak: and he will shew you things to come"* (John 16:13). The ability to wait and take instructions and guidance from the Holy Spirit before reaction is an evidence of self-control. To do well in faith, you must bear this great fruit of the Spirit and if you have not gotten this experience yet, pray and ensure you are filled as in the day of Pentecost to begin to experience the supernatural.

CHAPTER 9

THE SWEETNESS OF MEEKNESS

"The meek are those who quietly submit themselves to God, to His Word and to His rod, who follow His directions, and comply with His designs, and are gentle toward all men." —**Matthew Henry**

M eekness is a condition of being submissive to a constituted authority. *"Submit yourselves to every ordinance of man for the Lord's sake: whether it be to the king, as supreme; Or unto governors, as unto them that are sent by him for the punishment of evildoers, and for the praise of them that do well"* (1 Peter 2:13-14). Meekness as a part of the fruit of the Holy Spirit is total submission to a divine authority empowered by the indwelling power of the Holy Spirit in a believer.

John Piper once said that *"Meekness begins when we put our trust in God."* The ability to submit to the laws of men genuinely and totally is predicated on total submission to the divine authority. When you are submissive to God, He empowers you by His Holy Spirit to be submissive to the authority of men instituted by God. Where there is submission, peace reigns because things work out well for mutual good. You may disagree with government policies, but submissiveness, regardless of your opinion is a tribute to the divine authority that institutes every human government.

Jesus Christ was a great symbol of meekness. He had everything it took to contend His execution by the Jewish authority, but He was calm and submissive onto death. The meekness of Christ was required by two different authorities; to the Jewish laws, He was a convicted criminal and to the divine laws He was a reconciler. The message of meekness of Christ even onto death reveals total submission to God and absolute trust for His will and divine intervention. *"And he was withdrawn from them about a stone's cast, and kneeled down, and prayed, Saying, Father, if thou be willing, remove this cup from me: nevertheless not my will, but thine, be done"* (Luke 22:42-43).

The act of meekness could be painful, but the ability to easily absorb the pains is gained through salvation and sanctification. Meekness as a Fruit of the Holy

Spirit protects against the penalties of laws. People find it difficult submitting to constituted authorities because they lack submissiveness to divine laws. It is lack of submissiveness that makes an individual to intentionally violate laws such as running a stop sign, red light or driving above speed limit. An individual that is submissive to God is regulated by the Holy Spirit and obeys natural laws and is thereby immune to the penalties of Human laws. *"... against such there is no law"* (Galatians 5: 23b).

Meekness is the character that gives you the discipline required to be successful where others are failing, because it involves transparency and selflessness. The most important resource to any successful business is human capital (People) and leadership commitment is a great inspiration to earn loyalty of the human capital. One thing many of the world's most successful people have in common is meekness; the ability to inspire others. Now that we understand the concept of meekness (submissiveness) let us here examine its importance in everyday living.

MEEKNESS IN AUTHORITY

Submission to authority is an evidence of respect for the Giver of such authority. *"Let every soul be subject unto the higher powers. For there is no power but of God: the powers that be are ordained of God"* (Romans

13:1). Every constituted authority is an extension of divine authority intended to maintain law and order. The Ten Commandments provided the template and framework for the present day Western legal systems and Democracy.

Jesus demonstrated a good example of meekness by making Himself the fulfilment of the law and taught His disciples the true interpretation of the Ten Commandments. *"Think not that I am come to destroy the law, or the prophets: I am not come to destroy, but to fulfil. For verily I say unto you, Till heaven and earth pass, one jot or one tittle shall in no wise pass from the law, till all be fulfilled. Whosoever therefore shall break one of these least commandments, and shall teach men so, he shall be called the least in the kingdom of heaven: but whosoever shall do and teach them, the same shall be called great in the kingdom of heaven"* (Matthew 5:17-19).

It is worthy to note that Jesus Christ, our perfect Example is the fulfilment of the law and believers are expected to be submissive to the laws of the land as an evidence of genuine conversion. The only exception to the rule is when the authority is made to usurp the glory that is due for God, for it is written; *"I am the LORD: that is my name: and my glory will I not give to another, neither my praise to graven images"*(Isaiah 42:8).

Believers are to be submissive to the laws that promote spiritual values than those that promote lust and self at the expense of God. Daniel was a great example as a slave boy under the kingship of Babylonian king, Nebuchadnezzar. He was meek and submissive to the laws and rules of the land to the extent that they did not defile him. Daniel refused to defile himself with the king's food regardless of the fact that he was a stranger in the land of Babylon and the king had decreed that he and other boys be fed a portion of the king's meal. But why did Daniel refuse to comply with the king's decree? He understood that the king's meal was always sacrificed to their heathen gods and that eating it would defile him.

MEEKNESS IN LEADERSHIP

Meekness, an important Fruit of the Spirit is very essential for successful leadership. Effective leadership requires the ability to objectively reflect the interests and the inputs of followership. According to Rick Warren, *"meekness is not weakness but strength under control."* Every leader is given a certain degree of authority to implement his or her leadership responsibilities. A litmus test for a meek leader is the ability to put his or her powers under control. It takes a meek leader to earn the loyalty of followers. When a leader arrogates his or her will over the interests and opinions of others, he or she stands to lose the loyalty and respect of followers.

Meekness in leadership is fairness to all in execution of rules governing the organization, regardless of position or economic status, because it is the manifestation of the Spirit of God in a believer and He is no respecter of persons. *"Tribulation and anguish, upon every soul of man that doeth evil, of the Jew first, and also of the Gentile; But glory, honour, and peace, to every man that worketh good, to the Jew first, and also to the Gentile: For there is no respect of persons with God"* (Romans 2: 9-11).

A meek leader, at every level of leadership, must be submissive to God. He is the one who yields to the wishes and opinions of his followers over personal interest. A meek leader enjoys maximum cooperation from the followers for corporate success but a leader who rules with partiality will lose the respect and loyalty of his followers and fail. *"So when all Israel saw that the king hearkened not unto them, the people answered the king, saying, What portion have we in David? neither have we inheritance in the son of Jesse: to your tents, O Israel: now see to thine own house, David. So Israel departed unto their tents. But as for the children of Israel which dwelt in the cities of Judah, Rehoboam reigned over them"* (1 Kings 12: 16-17).

Rehoboam lost the loyalty of his followers in Israel

because he rejected their counsels and ruled with absolute powers. Notice that Rehoboam took the counsels of one school of thought at the expense of the others in his executive actions. With this singular action of his, Rehoboam edged God out of the equation, because there is no partiality with God. Rehoboam's leadership failure should be a lesson for leaders, especially those in spiritual leadership capacity. He was running a "divide and rule" system with a factionalized and polarized followership. And Scripture makes it clear that a kingdom divided against itself cannot stand (Mark 3:25).

It behooves a leader to harmonize different opinions of the followership with a win-win perspective instead of taking sides with one group. Abraham Lincoln acted on this Scripture and made a statement that resulted in the most powerful union in the history of man. *"A house divided against itself cannot stand. I believe this government cannot endure permanently, half slave and half free. I do not expect the Union to be dissolved – I do not expect the house to fall – but I do expect it will cease to be divided. It will become all one thing or all the other."* – Abraham Lincoln. A meek leader should always bear in mind that what unites people is always greater than what divides them. A spiritual leader whose congregation is afflicted with strife and division should check his or her meekness and submissiveness to God.

Apostle Paul identified division and strive in the Corinthian Church and strongly condemned same. *"And I, brethren, could not speak unto you as unto spiritual, but as unto carnal, even as unto babes in Christ. I have fed you with milk, and not with meat: for hitherto ye were not able to bear it, neither yet now are ye able. For ye are yet carnal: for whereas there is among you envying, and strife, and divisions, are ye not carnal, and walk as men? For while one saith, I am of Paul; and another, I am of Apollos; are ye not carnal? Who then is Paul, and who is Apollos, but ministers by whom ye believed, even as the Lord gave to every man? I have planted, Apollos watered; but God gave the increase. So then neither is he that planteth any thing, neither he that watereth; but God that giveth the increase. Now he that planteth and he that watereth are one: and every man shall receive his own reward according to his own labour"* (1 Corinthians 3:1-8).

Leadership meekness translates to organizational meekness. Meekness among organizational staff engenders unity and team work to enhance productivity. Every organizational leader's goal is to get the job done to maximize productivity, and meekness on the part of leadership is key. A meek leader is empowered by the Spirit of God with the compassion to motivate staff and celebrate work excellence without prejudice.

Abraham exemplified meekness when he asked his nephew, Lot to choose the location he wanted for his animals to graze, and he was ready to take the remaining portion of the land for his own animals. Abraham as the uncle of Lot had the opportunity to take the best portion of the grazing lands but was meek enough to surrender this opportunity to lot. When Abraham relocated from Egypt to Canaan with his nephew Lot, each of them was very rich in livestock and there was only a limited portion of land available to sustain both of their livestock because the native Canaanites occupied most of the available land. Abraham suggested separation between him and Lot, adding that if Lot chose to go left, he would go to the right.

In the spirit of meekness and submissiveness, Abraham yielded his opportunity to his nephew to avoid conflict and contention between his workers and those of Lot. *"And the land was not able to bear them, that they might dwell together: for their substance was great, so that they could not dwell together. And there was a strife between the herdmen of Abram's cattle and the herdmen of Lot's cattle: and the Canaanite and the Perizzite dwelled then in the land. And Abram said unto Lot, Let there be no strife, I pray thee, between me and thee, and between my herdmen and thy herdmen; for we be brethren. Is not the whole land before thee? separate thyself, I pray thee, from me: if thou wilt take the left hand, then I will go to the right; or if thou depart to the right hand, then I will go to the left"* (Genesis 13:6-9). One of the most important benefit of this Fruit of the Spirit is the ability of the bearer to resolve crisis amicably.

Moses was another leader that was meek, to the point that God testified of his meekness in the face of a heated criticism from his followers. He trusted God and God took vengeance on his behalf by afflicting Miriam with leprosy. Moses was able to let go of Miriam's offences and interceded for her healing. A meek leader easily forgives and gives opportunity for a second chance. *"And he said, Hear now my words: If there be a prophet among you, I the LORD will make myself known unto him in a vision, and will speak unto him in a dream. My servant Moses is not so, who is faithful in all mine house. With him will I speak mouth to mouth, even apparently, and not in dark speeches; and the similitude of the LORD shall he behold: wherefore then were ye not afraid to speak against my servant Moses? And the anger of the LORD was kindled against them; and he departed. And the cloud departed from off the tabernacle; and, behold, Miriam became leprous, white as snow: and Aaron looked upon Miriam, and, behold, she was leprous. And Aaron said unto Moses, Alas, my lord, I beseech thee, lay not the sin upon us, wherein we have done foolishly, and wherein we have sinned. Let her not be as one dead, of whom the flesh is half consumed when he cometh out of his mother's womb. And Moses cried unto the LORD, saying, Heal her now, O God, I beseech thee"* (Numbers 12:6-13).

Another individual whose meekness distinguished him as a great leader was Elisha the son of Shaphat. He was very submissive to the leadership of Elijah, and his meekness made him a worthy successor of Elijah upon whom Elijah's double portion was released. Elisha did not allow people to dissuade him from his loyalty to the leadership of Elijah and followed him until his ascension. *"And it came to pass, when they were gone over, that Elijah said unto Elisha, Ask what I shall do for thee, before I be taken away from thee. And Elisha said, I pray thee, let a double portion of thy spirit be upon me. And he said, Thou hast asked a hard thing: nevertheless, if thou see me when I am taken from thee, it shall be so unto thee; but if not, it shall not be so. And it came to pass, as they still went on, and talked, that, behold, there appeared a chariot of fire, and horses of fire, and parted them both asunder; and Elijah went up by a whirlwind into heaven. And Elisha saw it, and he cried, My father, my father, the chariot of Israel, and the horsemen thereof. And he saw him no more: and he took hold of his own clothes, and rent them in two pieces. He took up also the mantle of Elijah that fell from him, and went back, and stood by the bank of Jordan; And he took the mantle of Elijah that fell from him, and smote the waters, and said, Where is the LORD God of Elijah? and when he also had smitten the waters, they parted hither and thither: and Elisha went over"* (2 Kings 2:9-14).

Jesus Christ was an unparalleled icon of meekness. He was very submissive to God in His assignment as the Savior of the world. The journey to the cross was not easy for Him, but He was meek enough to offer Himself a sacrificial lamb to redeem the world. *"And he went a little further, and fell on his face, and prayed, saying, O my Father, if it be possible, let this cup pass from me: nevertheless not as I will, but as thou wilt"* (Matthew 26:39). Jesus the crucified was able to forgive his crucifiers because meekness is a manifestation of God's unconditional forgiveness. To be like Christ, we must allow God to take over our lives and we will manifest the Fruit of the Spirit.

MEEKNESS IN THE FAMILY

Every family that is founded on meekness and submissiveness will overcome every season of storm in Life. Jesus Christ admonished every family on the importance of submissiveness as a precursor for a joyful family. *"Wives, submit yourselves unto your own husbands, as unto the Lord. For the husband is the head of the wife, even as Christ is the head of the church: and he is the saviour of the body. Therefore as the church is subject unto Christ, so let the wives be to their own husbands in every thing. Husbands, love your wives, even as Christ also loved the church, and gave himself for it; That he might sanctify and cleanse it with the washing of water by the word, That he might present it to himself a glorious church, not having spot, or wrinkle, or any such thing; but that it should be holy and without blemish. So ought men to love their wives as their own bodies. He that loveth his wife loveth himself. For no man ever yet hated his own flesh; but nourisheth and cherisheth it, even as the Lord the church: For we are members of his body, of his flesh, and of his bones. For this cause shall a man leave his father and mother, and shall be joined unto his wife, and they two shall be one flesh. This is a great mystery: but I speak concerning Christ and the church. Nevertheless let every one of you in particular so love his wife even as himself; and the wife see that she reverence her husband"* (Ephesians 5:22-33).

Every family is expected to follow the pattern of Christ's submissiveness as the spiritual husband and the head of the church. For spouses to be successful in submission to marriage or family, they must be submissive first to God through salvation. You may fake submission in marriage, but it will not stand the test of time, because God cannot be faked. It is written; *"Every good gift and every perfect gift is from above, and cometh down from the Father of lights, with whom is no variableness, neither shadow of turning"* (James 1:17).

Meekness, otherwise called Submissiveness is an attribute of God and cannot be counterfeited, you can only manifest it when the Spirit of God in living inside of you. Some went into marriage with self-made meekness, but their union could not survive any stormy season of marriage. Notice that

Jesus recommends mutual submissiveness from all stakeholders in the interest of harmonious living. It then follows that both the husband and the wife are expected to be submissive to one another. *"Submitting yourselves one to another in the fear of God"* (Ephesian 5:21).

The absence of submission in marriage leads to various problems, because where there is no submission, love is absent, and in the absence of love, there is no marriage. There is no submission without love, and it is impossible to love without having the Spirit of God inside of you. The basic thing is knowing the God of love and letting Him work in you, and you will begin to manifest meekness and submissiveness to enable you enjoy your marital relationship. *"Beloved, let us love one another: for love is of God; and everyone that loveth is born of God, and knoweth God. He that loveth not knoweth not God; for God is love"* (1 John 4:7-8).

Submission is earned through love for each other; therefore, it is important for families that are founded on infatuated or fake love to make things right by inviting God in repentance into their family. When God takes over your family, you will begin to see the manifestation of His presence. When God is at the center of the family, there will be submission and where submission is present, there will be honor and prayers will be answered. *"Likewise, ye husbands, dwell with them according to knowledge, giving honour unto the wife, as unto the weaker vessel, and as being heirs together of the grace of life; that your prayers be not hindered"* (1 Peter 3:7).

Can you imagine praying for a breakthrough and nothing happens just because your marriage is not conditioned for honoring your wife. I recommend involving God in any family that are going through crisis and things will begin to work for good in such families. A functional family produces a functional community which in turn births a functional world where peace and orderliness will reign. Until we turn to the God of righteousness, there will be no manifestation of the Fruit of the Spirit to keep the world in peace. To usher in peace into our violent and crisis ridden world, we must yield to the God of peace at whose words every form of storm and crisis will cease.

summary

BEARING THE SPIRIT'S FRUIT IN BRIEF

- Love is the desire to go through painful experience with another without any compensation.

- God's love for the world costs Him giving His only begotten Son to bring eternal justification. He therefore desires for the people to love and live in love.

- The way you met God determines how far you will go with Him. Peter was easily and honorably invited, but easily denied Christ. Paul on the other hand was struck and forcefully drafted and still stuck with Christ through every stormy season of his ministry.

- The choice to let God into your life and live it for you is like hiring the manufacturer of your car to be your driver. If he or she remains your driver, you are guaranteed a sound and a healthy car.

- When you hand-over your life totally to God, you

are guaranteed a smooth ride in life; from labor to favor, from pain to gain, from shame to fame, from begging to giving, from picking to gleaning, from horror to honor, from intimidation to invitation, from pity to pretty.

- In a lust-driven Church there is division and discrimination, mostly along racial, ethnic, or sectional lines, motivated by mere social support system rather than godly and genuine love.

- In a lust-driven Church, people of like manner and interest gather themselves to gossip instead of fellowship, turning the Church into a theatre of hatred, strife and fighting over human recognitions.

- In the absence of love, the devil rejoices, because he is winning by accomplishing his mission.

- When you are a doer of God's word, He takes care of your adversaries before they start manifesting.

- I have not heard of any marriage without challenges but love and forgiveness can walk you through them all.

- For any marriage to be successful, both partners must first love God with all their souls, and He will bind them together with an unconditional love that cannot be broken by individual feelings and emotions.

- While feeling is based on perception, love is based on empathy.

- The younger generation must realize as intending couples that successful marriage is based on cherished similar values shared by both spouses; in this case, they both love God.

- Love is God bringing man back to Himself from conviction and condemnation for continuous purification and justification.

- Joy is not just the feeling of happiness and pleasures, but the expression of fulfilment derived from the hope and assurance of ending well with a resounding welcome home to live in eternity with God.

- When your spirit receives the signal of rebirth through salvation, you begin to experience the realm of overflowing joy beyond human comprehension.

- Patience is the vehicle that drives you to the end of all obstacles where all miracles begin.

- Patience simply means to endure pains of the present to ensure gains of the future.

- Failure is like the stop sign, but not the end of the journey. It is for you to stop for a minute, review your past and pre-view your future.

- The obstacles today work for the miracles tomorrow.

- Each one of us is made to be something through something, and until we go through something, we cannot be something. Going from something to the something through something of life requires diligence and resilience, by patience.

- Real failure is failing to work through failure until success is finally achieved.

- While compromise takes you farther away from your purpose, diligence and patience hasten your purpose to appear.

- Instead of casting the first stone at your offenders, be gentle enough to offer a second chance because no one is perfect.

- Gentleness does not cease to be kind to others even when they seem not to deserve it.

- Substantial faith is ignoring fear of the shadow to speak out the reality.

- Fear keeps you mute in situations to accept defeat, but faith keeps you vocal through situations to claim your victory.

- The substance of faith is hope in hopeless situations.

- Your spoken word of faith has the potential to uncover your hidden testimonies.

- Always learn to say "no" to obstacles as you walk the path of destiny to avoid stopping half-way to your destination where your miracles await you.

- The journey of destiny is time specific and it is the wings of patience that will fly you there safely.

- Self-control is the ability to correctly apply the word of God to situations in accordance with His will and purpose.

- Self-control affords a believer a lifestyle that can resist temptation and sin.

- Your daily decisions and actions are informed of the spirit that rules you.

- Self-control makes a good leader take responsibility for the failure of the organization and attribute success to his team.

- A good leader takes a little more than his share of the blame and a little less than his share of the credit (Arnold Glasow).

- Yelling makes your voice silence your words.

- Speak gently and quietly so your children can hear your words instead of your voice.

- Children subjected to frequent yelling end up with low self esteem and increased aggression towards others.

- The ability to wait and take instructions from the Holy Spirit before reactions to situations is the evidence of self-control.

- There are many reasons to give up on marriage vows, but a self-controlled life sees them as associated cost of relationships.

- Meekness begins when we put our trust in God (John Piper).

- When you are submissive to God, He empowers you to be submissive to the authority instituted by Him.

- Where there is mutual submission, peace reigns because things work out well for mutual good.

- Submission to constituted authority above opinion is a tribute to the divine authority.

- Being meek could be painful, but the ability to easily absorb pain is gained through salvation and sanctification.

- A meek person is regulated by the Holy Spirit to obey natural and human laws and is thereby immune to their penalties.

- One common thing among successful people is meekness, the ability to inspire others.

159

- Every constituted authority is an extension of divine authority intended to maintain law and order

- A family founded on meekness and submissiveness will overcome all stormy seasons in life.

- You may fake submission in marriage, but it will not stand the test of time because God cannot be faked.

- Meekness cannot be counterfeited; you can only manifest it when the Spirit of God dwells inside of you.

- Where there is no love, there is no mutual submission, and in the absence of mutual submission, there is no marriage.

- When God is at the center of the family, there will be submission and when submission is present, there will be honor and answered prayers.

- To usher in peace into our violent and crisis ravaged world, we must yield to the God of peace at whose words every form of storm ceases.

- Until we turn to the God of righteousness there will be no manifestation of the Spirit's Fruit to keep the world in peace.

www.ingramcontent.com/pod-product-compliance
Lightning Source LLC
LaVergne TN
LVHW051239080426
835513LV00016B/1663